GO BIG!

A BOSS Attitude for SUCCESS!

RENZIE L. RICHARDSON

Copyright © 2021
All Rights Reserved
ISBN: 978-1-7348186-4-2

DEDICATION

I dedicate this book to all the women, black and brown business owners, CEOs, and entrepreneurs who inspired and trusted me with their dreams, fears, vision, and goals they accomplished because they chose to GO BIG!

ACKNOWLEDGMENTS

Writing this book was more challenging than I thought but also rewarding as I learned so much about the success of women, black and brown entrepreneurs, business owners, and CEOs. None of this would have been possible without conversations with successful business owners that you may never see in a headline and reading countless stories about women, black and brown businesses who know the formula. They are growing and scaling their business.

I am so thankful for my clients who encourage me to share my passion for women, black and brown businesses, and why their success is vital to our economy and shifting policies that impact our success and wealth.

Next, I am so thankful for all the lessons I learned as an athlete. Mind you, I was at best a marginal player, but the lessons my coaches taught are embedded in who I am and how I apply them to my work, pushing the boundaries and believing in myself to be better than my best. And when I fall, get up and try again.

Lastly, I am so thankful for my three beautiful children – Erika, Daphne, and Quentin. I wish for you is to love, live and go for your dreams.

ABOUT THE AUTHOR

When I was downsized and forced to find a way to keep a roof over my head and food on the table, becoming a business owner was much faster than putting in a bunch of applications and waiting for a company to call to offer me a job. Besides, I was so tired of playing small to make people who held my livelihood in their hands feel big and powerful. I was tired of being silenced, marginalized, and excluded by department heads who had no interest in my abilities or sponsoring me for the next level up.

The answer for me was to start my own business – after all, how hard can it be? Well, it was not "easy" at all.

I was in a coffee café and overheard a conversation between two older men discussing *economic cycles, rising domestic products, tariffs, and favorable market indicators*. A few terms I knew "a little" about but not enough that I would bet a dollar.

This book is a compilation of what I know about business growth and profiles of successful women and minority-owned businesses. I also researched case studies to find advanced principles that are more than a notion of what business growth and scalability is and why it takes a BOSS attitude to GO BIG!

My mission is to help women and minority-owned businesses grow, starting with knowing their CEO traits, personal strengths, and what it takes to get to the next level.

As a business coach, I've enjoyed coaching and training women, minority business owners, and CEOs of multi-million-dollar corporations, helping them overcome obstacles that stood in the path of their success. Sometimes, my role was to help them make an *"attitude adjustment,"* and other times, it was pulling back the layers to unblock the path to success.

Despite our flaws and limited access to resources, grit, hustle, innovation, and faith kept us in a mighty way. Suppose we hold on to these traits and apply them to learning advanced business principles? I think we can create more than one million jobs, significantly impact the Gross Domestic Product (GDP), have a bigger seat at the table to change institutional policies that impact women and minority business growth and wealth-building. We can also affect economic growth on main streets and in black and brown communities across America. I hope this book inspires and gets you fired up to do BIG things with your business.

PREFACE

According to the Urban Dictionary and a few words of my own, here's the definition of a BOSS:

A person who knows what s/he wants knows how to get what s/he wants and gets it when s/he wants. S/he lives by their code of integrity and does not care about what others think. A BOSS has his or her own personality and does not follow the norm, just because it is the norm. A BOSS does not settle for less than what s/he is worthy of. A BOSS is driven and resilient.

They are competitive, have GRIT, and all of their actions aim to achieve a single-minded goal to take their place at the summit among all the winners who defied the odds to win – a BOSS!

A BOSS often denies that they are boss but know in their hearts that they are. They are driven by winning. They are leaders who mind their business, and they get things done. S/he is admired, and others are inspired to follow them.

A *BOSS* is **B**uilt **o**n **S**piritual **S**trength.

CONTENTS

Dedication .... *iii*
Acknowledgments .... *v*
About the Author .... *vii*
Preface .... *ix*

Chapter 1 – Introduction 1
Chapter 2 – Small but Mighty 15
Chapter 3 – The Big Picture 27
Chapter 4 – Your Product or Service 39
Chapter 5 – Managed Growth 61
Chapter 6 – Manage Stress on the Business 81
Chapter 7 – Cost to the Bottom Line 105
Chapter 8 – Resources for Growth 119
Chapter 9 – Talent for Growth 139
Chapter 10 – Investment in Growth 153
Chapter 11 – Part 1-Target KPIs for Growth 167
Chapter 11 – Part 2-Understanding of KPIs Through a Case Study 177
Chapter 12 – Part1- Making Tough Decisions for Growth 189
Chapter 12 – Part 2-Making Tough Decisions for Growth 197
Chapter 13 – Benchmarking The Growth 203
Chapter 14 – Breakthrough for Growth 211

CHAPTER 1
INTRODUCTION

Women and minority-owned businesses have perfected the game of hustle, bootstrapping, improvising, and *making ends meet*. One quote that says it best is from Reid Hoffman, co-founder of LinkedIn: *"An entrepreneur is someone who will jump off a cliff and assemble an airplane on the way down."* But for black women entrepreneurs, Dell Gines, author of a report from the Federal Reserve Bank of Kansas City, added while discussing *Black Women Business Startups,* "They do it with only a toothpick and a napkin." He meant to say that black women lack the resources and capital to launch their startups. However, they continue to leave indelible impressions in business by building their enterprises from scratch.

The 2018 State of Women-Owned Business Report commissioned by American Express stated that the number of women-owned businesses grew an impressive 58% from 2007 to 2018. The number of companies owned by black women grew by an astonishing 164%. That's good. That's good. Impressive! However, entrepreneurs, solopreneurs, and minority business owners of today still need a push, a motivational push to elevate the game and scale their business to be a seven-figure enterprise. Besides believing in their abilities, unapologetically, I found in my work as a business coach that they need insights and a formula to scale and sustain their business.

Deciding to take a leap of faith to start a business, I remember the number of times a feeling of trepidation and doubt consumed me. When you think about starting a business, your head is bouncing all over the place and pondering all the aspects for a successful start, growing your business, and then sustaining it over time – it is enough to make you feel woozy! It's common for some budding entrepreneurs to feel stressed about the lack of resources. Still, the key to a successful business is that you must never give up and see yourself in the future running a successful business. I can assure you that you will pray for a miracle to get you through a rough spot, but never give up. Tough times strengthen and sharpen your edge to wear the shoes of a BOSS – one who does not settle for less than what he or she is worthy of.

When Gines talked about black women building startups with a toothpick and a napkin, he meant to make us aware of a reality that we cannot run away from - the reality that the world isn't fair. We are fighting to be a part of an economy that is not inclusive for all. It gives more to some and nothing to others. However, while we complain about it, courageous women embark on their success journey with nothing but a dream and their will to do something big. We usually launch our startups with personal savings, a side gig, our main gig, or an investment from the family, friends, or the neighborhood shark for most women business owners. In such circumstances, the thought of giving up and abandoning your goals might cross your mind daily, but the hustle and reaching out to help define your determination and the future of your business. And so, whether you are a *sistah*, trying to kick-start your business, or you are already a small business owner, looking to scale it, being agile and playing BIG are the first steps to take your business to the next level.

According to the United States Census Bureau data, the number of firms owned by women has doubled in numbers for the last two decades. The numbers mean they are taking risks despite ranking at the very bottom of the big bank lists. Women business owners and aspiring entrepreneurs come across countless rejections and criticisms at the start of business ownership. Still, the fact that many of them succeed in becoming great business owners is what you should focus on if you want to succeed as a woman entrepreneur or solopreneur. Come to think of it, struggle and rejection are also important. They're sort of essential for growth to build a multimillion-dollar company. Maybe that's why they say: dream big but start small.

Significance of Dreaming Big but Starting Small

Don't shy away from starting small. If you are ambitious and your goals are equally ambitious, be prepared for challenges to come your way. Rejections will come your way. If you dream of playing in the big leagues by making your business a seven-figure enterprise, then continue dreaming and see yourself three years, then seven years into the future – *if you can't see where you are in the future, it's unlikely you will get there.* Believe it or not, having the vision to achieve your dream can start with a pebble that grows to be the size of a stone - the key to achieving those dreams is starting small.

Starting small helps you break down that huge goal into small, manageable action steps. It helps you stay focused. Let's use the running analogy here. It's like running marathons. When you run, there are mile marks along the path – one, two, five, ten. So when you run and reach those mile marks, you feel happy, focused, and driven because you're making progress, you're moving forward, and there's just no way you're going to give up because you've gotten so far. The same thing happens with you when you set big business goals and start small. You stay focused because you know where you need to go, and you can measure how much progress you're making, despite setbacks and detours.

Starting small gives you clarity. Let's say you have this big ambitious goal, but you have no clue how to get there. It's like you want to drive to New York City overnight in complete darkness. You drive and can only see 300 feet ahead of you, but by the time you get to that point, you see another 300 feet, and so you just keep moving forward. The next thing you know, by the morning, you have reached your destination. The same thing applies to your goals. You go as far as you can see, and you can see so much further when you get there. As a result, you just keep moving forward.

One of the biggest reasons people quit on their big goals is that they become discouraged. You get disappointed when you see no progress. Starting small assures that you are making progress and you don't quit. It gives you the enthusiasm you need to keep going. Also, when you start small, the impossible becomes possible. Many entrepreneurs think that they have to get lucky or need to have everything right to make their startup successful, but that's not the case. Achieving small in the beginning will lead you to reach your audacious goals in the end.

When you start small, you become an inspiration to others. By your actions, you will inspire your friends, family, and your community to take action and start the business they want to do in life, nurture it, and transform it into a multi-million-dollar venture. It's how you start small and chase your big dream that sets an example.

Many minority entrepreneurs of the past started small as many entrepreneurs and solopreneurs are doing today. All they had was a spark or idea in mind. They strived, struggled, took risks, and faced challenges, only to become a force to be reckoned with. Your side-hustle can take you to big things. Some of these entrepreneurs include:

Robert S. Abbot

The founder of *The Chicago* Defender, today known as a Chicago-based online African-American newspaper, started his business with just 25 cents in his pocket, a great vision in his mind, and a willingness to grow. As minor as his initial investment was, his dreams were bigger than that. Back in 1905, Abbot printed 300 copies of his paper from the kitchen of his landlord's apartment and soon became the owner of an influential African-American newspaper, which was considered the *most important* newspaper of its kind. He started his enterprise by himself and hired the first paid employee in 1910, after running his enterprise for five years, all by himself.

If Robert S. Abbot kept thinking that 25 cents were not enough to start a business he wanted to do, he would never have seen success. He took a risk and invested all that he had to create an enterprise without anyone's support: no finances, no employee, nothing. But still, he succeeded. How? By believing in his ideas and taking risks without hesitation.

Madam C.J. Walker

Madam C.J. Walker was the first black woman to have followed her business dream. Despite living her life as a laundress and working for just a dollar, she was determined and wanted to provide the best for her daughter. Madam Walker faced problems related to hair loss and dandruff, which led her to develop her hair products. With an investment of a mere $1.25, she began manufacturing her products in a washtub and soon became the first self-made female millionaire in the U.S. During an interview, she stated that the idea of her product and what to mix in it had appeared to her in a dream.

Daymond John

Daymond Garfield John, now known as an American businessman, author, investor, and motivational speaker, started from waiting tables at a restaurant, handing out flyers on the street, and finally coming up with an idea of starting his clothing company. In 1992, with his two friends, John decided to make hats for youngsters. With only 40 dollars in their hands, they purchased fabric, learned to sew from his mother, and turned those 40 dollars into a brand worth $6 billion today. John's mother allowed his son and his friends to take over her house and use it to expand their business. They didn't ask for finance from banks or investors. They simply worked it out with whatever they had and succeeded in making billion-dollar sales. Their brand, FUBU, soon got recognized as one of the largest clothing brands in the U.S. In 1994, FUBU received $300,000 worth of orders and went on to make $350 million in revenue in later years.

John served as the catalyst in his group for making his ideas and dreams a reality. What started as a source for *easy money* now stands as a company that continues to grow and helps other small businesses achieve their dreams by investing in them.

Cashmere Nicole

A single mother and a breast cancer survivor, Cashmere Nicole founded her brand called Beauty Bakerie in 2011. She introduced lipsticks that were vegan, non-toxic, and cruelty-free. She has become a rare black woman to have raised $10 million from many big investors. She says, *"America is at an interesting inflection point, and now is a time for everyone to create change and a lasting legacy."*

However, Nicole's success didn't come to her as easily as it seems. When she was 10-year-old, she found herself reading business books and finding ways to create something for herself someday. She organized lemonade stands at the age of eight and wanted to become a teen entrepreneur, but things changed when she became a mother. Instead of reading about business growth and development, she started working multiple jobs to provide for her daughter and spent years with her dream suppressed in the corner of her mind. When she found herself somewhat financially stable, she began working for her brand and invested $50 in a simple Instagram advertisement, which didn't make any difference. She was 22 at the time.

During her years battling breast cancer, her brand started to deteriorate. However, soon her brand caught big investors' eye, like Unilever, that saw potential in her brand and invested money in it. Today, Nicole's brand is sold overseas in the United Kingdom and Germany. Celebrities wear her brand and promote it as well. Although her business seems to have found the light that she wanted, she continues to struggle each day, making her business better and bigger.

There will not be enough for you in the future if you do not believe in yourself, your ideas, and your business today. Like these people, many have struggled, not only in their initial phases but also throughout their business journeys. The struggle doesn't seem to stop for minorities and small business owners even when they reach a certain height of success.

However, the only thing that must always remain constant is belief. Your belief in your business idea and vision will help you become strong-willed.

To give you a hint about what believing in yourself, your business, or your ideas can do, here are some globally renowned personalities who started as small, unpopular people, but now they own million-dollar companies.

Jennifer Lopez

From being called stupid when expressing her desire to become a movie star to becoming an American actress, singer, dancer, fashion designer, producer, and businesswoman, Jennifer Lopez struggled a lot. She first discovered her desire to become an actress while auditioning for a low-budget movie called *My Little Girl*. After this, she showed her interest in similar things but got shut down by her parents, who said, "No Latino ever did that."

After leaving her parents' home and living by herself, she started working as a dancer in different musicals until she got her first-ever high-profile job as a fly girl in a famous T.V. show called *In Living Colors*.

When a movie named Selena became her breakthrough in the industry, she became the first-ever Hispanic actress to be paid as high as $1 million for her first salary. She utilized her position in the entertainment industry and released her first-ever album, which managed to top the charts. She then stepped into the business realm and invested in her clothing line and cosmetics brand, providing beauty products to women of all colors and sizes.

"You have to remember the value of your individuality—that you have something different and special to offer that nobody else can," Lopez said in an interview. This statement's reality is reflected in the journey that her career has been her whole life. She didn't settle for less. The show that granted her first solo performance was fairly famous, but she decided to part her ways to become something else. When she got her acting break, she didn't stop there either. She continued to hustle and decided to grow in a different arena.

"Used to have little, now I have a lot," Jennifer says in her famous song, *"Jenny from the Block,"* which talks about where she came from and how she became what she is today. She worked hard and moved from one thing to another to find what works best. After launching her fashion brand, which got more attention in the following years, Jennifer expanded it by adding sportswear for women as well as housing décor. In the second year of her business venture, she introduced a fragrance brand that became the best-selling celebrity brand of all time.

By achieving success in every business avenue, she tried her luck in, Jennifer Lopez has proven to be an entrepreneurial enigma with relentless vision. She utilized her intelligence and her immensely gravitated strategies to build and manage her brands magnificently. She grabbed every opportunity that came her way and broke all racial barriers to become the most influential Hispanic performers in the United States.

Kobe Bryant

The legacy of Kobe Bryant goes beyond the basketball court. Besides being a famous and brilliant basketball player, he was also known as an investor, a coach, and a brand-builder. Like J. Lo, Bryant diversified his career and stepped into the business world by co-founding Bryant Stibel, a venture capital firm in partnership with Jeff Stibel, the founder of Web.com. Although Bryant was a co-founder, the company recognized him as more than that. His visions and creative thinking led him to be an accomplished investor and entrepreneur. He transformed the skills that he used on the court and turned it into a successful business model. His firm invested in technology, data, and media companies and has assets worth more than $2 billion.

Bryant's journey as a basketball player gave him enough fame and success, but what made him enter this different arena? He could have stayed in court, playing basketball or training people, but he decided to implement his vision of helping others grow. In a CNBC interview, he stated that even though the returns are an essential factor, entrepreneurs' growth is also a significant aspect. Thus, Bryant Stibel invested in companies like Epic Games, Dell, and Alibaba. He also invested in Body armor; a sports drink maker. On top of all that, he founded Granity Studios, a media company.

As much as we like watching Bryant shooting the shots, he liked winning each game he played. But when he couldn't, he practiced till the sun came up. HHis determination and resolute sense made him a successful basketball player and entrepreneur.

Michael Jordan

Considered *too short* to play varsity basketball at the beginning of his career, Michael Jordan is the owner of Jordan Brand, which generates billions of dollars today. He was considered the first NBA player to become a billionaire and was named the *Business Person of the Year* for 2014 by Charlotte Business Journal.

One of the greatest, if not the greatest, player ever to play basketball, Michael Jordan was a boy whose father was only 5'9" and mother was 5'6". Never in his dreams had he thought of becoming an NBA player, especially when he could not play with his school basketball team. Jordan often locked himself in his room out of disappointment. However, he never gave up, neither on his height nor on his dream of becoming an NBA player.

In high school, as a sophomore, Jordan was 5'11", which is a pretty decent height, but he wanted so much more from life than this. His wish to be tall enough to play basketball was granted when he was in his junior year of high school. Michael grew up and became 6'3" tall. Later, he added three more inches to his height and stood at 6'6". The rest of his basketball career is known by everyone. The type of player he was and the revolution he brought to the game with his skills is not needed to be told. His name is enough.

Michael Jordan is one of the wealthiest athletes in the world. He may not have played professional basketball in decades, yet he makes crazy amounts of money on business ventures and endorsement deals. It all started back in 1984 when Jordan was a rookie and just beginning to get a nose for business. He signed an endorsement deal with Nike for $250,000 a year. Today, he has an estimated annual earning with Nike of $130 million. The Jordan Brand signature line sells more shoes and apparel than any other NBA player. These sales bring in more than $3 billion in annual revenue for the footwear giant.

In the 90s, Jordan endorsed various brands, like Gatorade. He still works with Hanes, earning over $14 million for promoting underwear. Jordan has also maintained a lucrative deal with Upper Deck valued at

$13 million from the sports trading card company. He is the fourth richest African-American as of 2019, with a net worth of $2.1 billion. He co-owns an automotive group, a steakhouse, and several other restaurants. His newest venture is with Cincoro Tequila.

The struggles and experiences of these people, how they started from nothing and ended up being multi-millionaires and billionaires, are nothing more than a guide for aspiring minority business owners. It's up to them to learn from the lives of such exemplary figures and seek inspiration to set an example of their own.

The Tenacity of Women-Owned Businesses

"Whatever the mind can conceive and believe, it can achieve."
-*Napoleon Hill*

When we talk about successful businesses, we tend to ignore the years of struggle that women business owners went through. For sure, one thing that keeps a business going is the consistency and perseverance of its owners. From all the personalities discussed in this chapter, not one stepped back from their vision even when they failed several times. When JLo's first few songs didn't garner much acclaim, when Kobe missed his most confident shots, when Jordan got rejected for being too short, they didn't stop chasing their dreams. They continued to pursue their goals without losing spirit and confidence.

Women who started from nothing and ended up becoming millionaires without any financial support, like Madam C.J. Walker and Cashmere Nicole, remind us that a tenacious and determined attitude is what pays off in the end. It's what makes you expand your business and go on to play the game on a bigger scale.

As women business owners/entrepreneurs, having a BOSS attitude, the heart of determination, and unwavering focus to build your business from the ground up are what it takes to overcome stereotypes and attitudes. From our past, the minorities who have made their journey have become the mentors for future entrepreneurs, offering great lessons drawn from their experiences. If these inspirational examples will help you kick-start your business or entrepreneurial venture, stay motivated, and never let anything hold you back. Have faith in your vision and ideas to have something different and unique to offer to people. In all honesty, that's the tried and tested way to do your part to build a more inclusive economy for everyone.

CHAPTER 2
SMALL BUT MIGHTY

"From a tiny spark may burst a mighty flame."
-Dante Alighieri

A business may be small, yet it can significantly impact the local economy and even the world. With that being said, running and maintaining a small business is by no means an easy task or less of a responsibility than running and maintaining a big business. Bigger brands can easily overshadow your business any given day with their influential position, a position that they have maintained for several years. But if you consider your business's size to be your biggest weakness, then you are wrong. You can certainly be a force to be reckoned with for your competitors, big and small.

With an unshakable belief in your small business's vision, why you started it, and the purpose it serves in creating jobs and contributing to the economy, the impact can be tangible and meaningful. Today, small businesses on the main street and those tucked away in urban communities offer more value to the local economy. Technology has also reimagined the way of doing business completely, regardless of its size – from online retail e-commerce to using artificial intelligence to predict consumer buying habits. Whether a small business is local or global, it has the edge over the Fortune companies because they are a close-knit network. As a business coach, I have seen so many small companies scale to the next level and be mighty and powerful because:

1. They understand the value of each employee.

2. They know that they have to support each other for their business to grow.

3. They have a personable approach to reach their customers and small enough to tailor consumer strategies with a personal touch.

4. They create more jobs than large employers and contribute to the economy's growth by introducing innovative ideas and hiring people who may not fit well in big corporations.

5. They offer a unique advantage over big businesses by attracting raw talent that the big companies overlook because they don't fit the corporate mold.

6. In today's economy, small businesses offer workers a meaningful way to work, and far more than a paycheck.

In today's U.S. economy, small business owners are the ones who yield creativity and provoke innovative thinking. Unlike big businesses, many small businesses say 'no' to politics, hierarchies, discrimination, and red tape. Instead, they are the tapestry of local urban vibes and emphasize hard work and perseverance to accomplish goals.

So, if you own a small business, understand that your business's size does not define its worth, but the number of jobs created carries more value. For a small business, such as a corner java shop or a hi-tech company in Silicon Valley, the opportunities to build wealth and create jobs are more prevalent with opportunities for small businesses to thrive.

The emphasis on *the bigger, the better* has shifted to *small but mighty, and small is "mo" better.* What matters is your business's story and the passion you want to build a company that offers a unique experience that differentiates you from corporate giants. I believe that each of us has talents like Madame C.J. Walker, Michael Jordan, and Jennifer Lopez. You just have to find that within your constitution and make use of your dream to be an entrepreneur with a business that is part of the backbone of a thriving U.S. and local economies. Aspiring women and minority entrepreneurs consider big businesses and multinational companies as threats because of their big brand reputation and the fact that they have unlimited resources, but you have an advantage.

Small business owners fail to realize that the big players are slow to embrace fresh ideas, mindset, and change just as much as they are of their position, worth, and reputation in the market. The thing is, the honchos of big corporations do not possess the passion and drive that women and minority business owners of today have. It's true that when the small business owners desire to get contract opportunities with the large Fortune 500 companies and look to them as a blueprint to earn millions.

Still, I think women and minority-owned businesses should look at ways to collaborate to create big ideas that elevate their contributions to economic development, jobs, and stability of local economies that benefit ecosystems that provide resources communities depend upon to thrive. The time has come for small businesses, entrepreneurs, and solopreneurs to understand their value and their collective power that is mightier than big established corporations. Your significance is broad and deep.

The Significance of Small Businesses

When I say the word *business*, what comes to your mind? You probably think of certain brands or companies you interact with every day, like Walmart, Apple, General Motors, etc. These companies are considered big businesses that employ thousands of people all across the country. If they decide to set up physical stores, they can provide hundreds of jobs to local communities. But unfortunately, big businesses are often vulnerable to changing market conditions and economic cycles, leading to widespread job loss or even recession. If big companies pose such a big risk, should communities look up to them for stability? What if a small business, more than a big business, holds the future for economic growth?

Small businesses include companies with anywhere from one to 500 employees. But don't let the numbers fool you because a small business is more important than you think. You see, small businesses make up 99.7% of all U.S. employer firms and businesses, with less than 20 workers making up 89.6%. The 28 million small businesses in America account for 54% of all U.S. sales. So, it's clear that small companies significantly impact the economy.

We hear a lot about large companies in the news, but small business is the engine of the U.S. economy. America is home to more than 28 million small businesses that employ 57 million workers. When you add owners and employees together, that's a community of roughly 85 million hardworking Americans dependent on a small business's success. These findings constitute most of the private-sector workforce. Small business owners are America's most important job creators. U.S. small businesses accounted for almost two-thirds of the net new jobs created between 1993 and 2013—a total of 11.8 million new career opportunities. In 2012, small businesses created more than 2.1 million net new jobs. Small businesses are the country's leading job creators because they are often growing and looking for new markets. To do so, they need additional employees along the way. On the other hand, large businesses generally stay the same size and hire new employees to replace departing ones.

However, high taxes and recent government regulations in health care, finance, and labor disproportionately hurt small businesses and prevent them from growing and adding new jobs to the economy. Big companies with big profits can afford to comply with red tape in a way that small businesses that are just starting cannot. As a result, small businesses still haven't entirely recovered from the Great Recession, as is showed by the chronically weak labor market. More than 94 million Americans are not working or actively looking for jobs. The labor force participation rate, which measures the percentage of employees and job-seekers in the U.S., is less than 63 percent, the lowest figure since the late 1970s. To bring small businesses back and strengthen the job market, job-killing taxes and regulations must be rolled back. Job creators should be encouraged to hire more employees, not forced to reduce career opportunities. With 85 million people depending on a small business's success, it's easy to see why small business is too big to fail.

Many people consider the economy to be led by big bad wolves, i.e., big corporations, but what they fail to see is that small business fortify the economy and make it stronger. As mentioned before, small businesses act as the economic engine because every new startup creates job opportunities. Similarly, small minority businesses contribute heavily to the strengthening of the economy as they are agile and can acclimate themselves to the changing market conditions. To get this message across clearly, let's take a look at how small business makes the economy strong.

Employment

Small businesses are crucial for job creation. Since the 1970s, they have provided 55% of all jobs and 66% of all net new jobs. Since 1990, while big businesses have eliminated four million jobs, small businesses have added eight million jobs.

Small business is a vital part of any community and a viable alternative to big business. Women and minority-owned small businesses bring creativity and growth to their community. For example, I met a black female entrepreneur who uses fruit and veggie peels, hulls, and leftovers to repurpose them into skincare products, such as masks, lotions, and acne treatment. She employs a team of people who possess the drive and passion for innovative ideas and invent unique solutions to existing problems. Perhaps that's the reason why large businesses buy out small businesses to infuse their brand with new products that are organic and grassroots. One of the stories that explain this kind of deal is when L'Oréal USA purchased Carol's Daughter, which offered a line of ethnic hair care products. L'Oréal USA's purchase gave the big corporate brand access to a multi-cultural consumer segment, also known as a rapidly expanding market that represents a significant growth opportunity in the beauty industry. The acquisition of Carol's Daughter offered L'Oreal USA a chance to expand its brand to include multi-culture consumer products.

An advantage that small businesses have that makes them attractive to creative, hi-tech job seekers is the opportunity to work in an environment that allows for freedom to innovate and do work that is meaningful and aligns with their values. In small business, employees have an opportunity to thrive in work environments that allows for diverse thinking styles and flexible ways of contributing value to the organization. The freedom to innovate and create new things helps boost retention while attracting young professionals to find comfortable work styles that match their values. More people become attracted to such firms and approach them willingly. There is no doubt that large companies maintain their space and press, but small business employees hold a big share of employment income. That's because small businesses operate locally. They create local jobs for people who do not wish to commute to other cities to seek employment and prefer hiring people from their community or territory. Small businesses create every two out of three new private-sector jobs. This explains that small businesses create jobs but also provide job satisfaction to their employees.

The challenge for women and black-owned business owners is to increase the number of jobs and economic development that grows and stabilizes communities.

According to an article by Blended Media – "Are We There Yet?" the author pointed out that Data from the Small Business Administration indicated that just over 19 million businesses, or 70.9 percent of all U.S. businesses, are white-owned. Blacks own about 2.6 million businesses or 9.5 percent of all U.S. businesses, and Latinos own 3.3 million businesses or 12.2 percent of all-American companies. But the sales and employment numbers told a more depressing story. The 19 million white-owned companies have 88 percent of the overall sales and control 86.5 percent of U.S. employment. In contrast, black businesses have a mere 1.3 percent of total American sales and 1.7 percent of the nation's employees. Latino businesses have 4 percent of U.S. sales and 4.2 percent of U.S. employment.

So, how do minority business owners Go Big to bend this curve?

Adaptable to Changes

When I started my business in 2008, like most entrepreneurs, I leveraged my diverse skill set to market potential people who were willing to invest their money with me – this is the art of the hustle, grit, and grind. Sometimes, when you are a small business owner, you get in where you can and look for the low hanging fruit.

Small businesses hold a unique ability to adapt to economic changes quickly. For starters, they do not have big bucks deals like large businesses. In other words, the hustle, grit, and grind teaches you valuable lessons about how to pivot in a time of economic crisis. Unlike large corporations, small businesses do not fall prey to drastic market decline where big companies downsize, furlough employees, and fall into the pit of recession. In challenging economic times, many women and minority-owned small businesses bear the decline because they are used to surviving with little cash or funds. In harsh economic times, sometimes small businesses experience a decline in customer spending, but their loyalty remains strong based on relationship and customer service. This, in turn, keeps the small business intact with their community and maintains the local economy.

Local Government Taxes

When small businesses thrive, they produce significant revenue and pay higher taxes. According to blndedmedia.com, the majority (57.9

percent) of businesses with paid employees had annual sales of more than $249,999. Therefore, there are economic reasons to support small businesses to increase retail, payroll taxes, and sales taxes to circulate in the local community to invest in local schools, economic development programs, and municipalities. A successful small business increases property value in a community, generating more property taxes for the local government. A great way to keep the dollars within the local economy is by supporting women and minority entrepreneurs and solopreneurs. These reasons improve and develop the local communities as a result.

Growth to a Corporation

In the previous chapter, we discussed well-known personalities and business owners who started very small but ended up running some of the most influential and prominent businesses of the 21stcentury. Their stories tell us that *small* businesses *do not* have to remain small. The tiny spark eventually turns into a fiery flame, attracting hundreds of customers and clients. Large companies like TLC Beatrice International, Worldwide Technology, and Vista Equity Partners also started as small businesses and grew into billion-dollar groundbreaking brands of all time. Many now-famous companies and enterprises started as nobodies but are now some of the world's leading companies. Their stories and many more stories like theirs tell us that you can expand your small business if you focus and be tenacious.

When small businesses grow and expand into more prominent entities, they tend to make their headquarters within the communities where they first started their business. When *small businesses turned large* and decide to establish their headquarters in their home communities, it helps other local women and minorities to kick-start their small businesses, which eventually transforms into big companies. Atlanta, Georgia, known as "*the city too busy to hate*," is the home of many successful million-dollar businesses, such as Moody Construction and Sons, Inc., Citizen's Trust Bank, and Wade Ford Inc. This chain leads to more employment opportunities, stimulates the local economy, and creates a market that helps develop future small businesses.

Healthy Competition

While many business owners wish to have no competitors, healthy competition is vital for small minority businesses. Why? Because to achieve a higher level of success, a certain level of competition becomes necessary. I grew up playing sports and became a fan of the National Basketball Association – the NBA. My favorite players were Michael Jordan and Kobe Bryant. Anyone could say the teams didn't need great players because of these two superstars. Over the years, these players inspired new players like LeBron James, Seth Curry, and Zion Williamson. Like sports, the lack of competition makes businesses static, and they remain satisfied with what they have instead of reaching for more. Companies with no competition will soon find no reason for improving their products/services. Many small businesses become a job for the entrepreneur or the business owner to cover living expenses. But with a considerate level of competition, small minority business owners thrive when driven and make an effort to compete and win. They learn how to up their game and provide services or products that exceed their competitors' offerings.

By healthy competition, I mean the kind of competition that urges your small business to thrive and inspires you to keep your eye on the prize – stay focus on the big picture. A lukewarm approach to competition only corrupts your beliefs and passion for your business, making you lose not only momentum but potentially your customers and footprint in your local community as well. Healthy competition helps create competitive, innovative, and diverse products and services, making competing businesses strive to achieve nothing less than the very best. In turn, the competition will boost the local economy by a considerable margin.

Diversity in Small Business

In today's economy, white male small business dominates this sector. However, diversified small companies have a chance to prosper and succeed and compete with white males and large corporations. When more women, ethnic, and racial minorities come together to build a company, human capital tends to grow substantially. McKinsey and Company's study shows that women's overall share of labor in the U.S. went from 37% of jobs to 47% over the past 40 years, accounting for a quarter of the current GDP. A diverse group can help the business by capturing a bigger share of a diverse consumer market. If companies keep adapting to the changes and accepting the diverse communities as owners and workers, then the economy will grow unprecedentedly.

Women of color now own 1.9 million firms in the U.S., which means that business owners' diversity helps the growth of the economy and employment. Small minority-owned businesses, especially businesses owned by women of color, generate $165 billion annually and annually employ 1.2 million people. By capitalizing on diverse communities' talents and hard work, countries can become more competitive in the global economy.

Running a small minority business asks a lot from its owners – you need to have an attitude like a *BOSS*. Your minority business needs to stand out from the crowd regardless of its size. While trying to stand out, make sure that you DO NOT look up to those big corporations that seem to rule the world. Look up to those businesses with a rich tapestry of overcoming adversity, those that have taken lemons and made lemonade. Or, look at those who similar in size and starting to scale their business to the next level. Learn from their resilience and bravery to stay in the game and be as visible as possible. If you want to stand out and maintain a good reputation for your business, be yourself, remain authentic and transparent to both your business and the people associated with it.

Let your tiny spark burst into flames by believing in the vision you have in your mind and staying passionate about your business despite its current size and position in the market. Believe it or not, and remember what I say, one day your business will grow to be an enterprise and become a force to be reckoned with in your market.

An oak tree starts with a seed, and roots grow deep, and the limbs spread wide.

CHAPTER 3
THE BIG PICTURE

As a small business owner, one of the most significant characteristics you need to possess is the capacity to plan for an extraordinary future by planning and thinking big. While having talented people in your business is crucial in achieving your goals, having exceptional talent to help shape the business's fate is equally important. These characteristics make the ultimate difference between a successful business's widely recognized name/brand and a company that operates like an abbreviation of one.

Have you ever thought about the reason why such a significant number of small businesses continuously battle to make ends meet while big ones seem to flourish? Why do some entrepreneurs appear to have a life luxurious enough to go on expensive vacations once or maybe twice a year, while others work exhaustingly long hours and end up making any significant growth in their businesses? One of the primary differences between a good and a great company is the *mindset;* the entrepreneur or solopreneur practice level keeps their attention on the business's big picture every day. To grow into a seven-figure business, small business owners need to establish a vision at the very start of their venture and set out to achieve that vision by adhering to a carefully laid out plan.

Importance of Setting a Vision and Growth Strategy

The inability to plan for the future can result in unavoidable failures for small businesses. The term *big picture* is regularly used in the business world but is applied effectively by companies only once in a while. Planning is why some businesses hire experts who specialize in setting a business vision. While most of the experts offer to write a strategic plan for your business, they do not generally appreciate the personal story behind your vision and your "why."

"For the vision is yet for an appointed time, but at the end, it shall speak, and not lie: though it tarry, wait for it; because it will surely come, it will not tarry." -Habakkuk 2:3, King James Version

If you are a small business owner, hiring an expert may be out of the question. Most small business owners have to establish a vision on their own at the beginning of their entrepreneurial journey and plan their growth strategy to keep track of their vision. Usually, a growth strategy begins by distinguishing what makes your business different and seizing your market opportunities. It goes past the advertising plans that guide you on meeting business targets. A growth strategy gives you a clear picture of how your business will advance to address today's difficulties, tomorrow, and far into the future.

Similarly, setting a vision is about setting goals or a statement of purpose that your business could use for settling on choices and plan a way of moving forward.

Every business ought to have a goal or focus that keeps advancing the vision over time. While this goal may be years or even decades away, it's fundamental that business owners are consistently keeping the future in perspective and marching on where they want to be, let's say, ten years down the road. Planning for the years ahead can be precarious for even the most eager entrepreneur, but this is where the idea of vision setting becomes an integral factor for building a sustainable business where objectives/strategies and visions set the way for what's to come. While vision and growth strategies can change as the business evolves, they still are the anchors for where your center of focus ought to be.

Having growth strategies are significant because they help you set objectives that are way ahead of what's going on in the market today. These strategies keep the employees and leaders engaged and inspire them to see ahead and plan for the future. Business owners and entrepreneurs make terrible choices frequently when their vision is shortsighted and limited based on options available today. Think about basing your decisions on emerging opportunities that will be available shortly. That is why both vision and growth strategies are essential for the business.

When You Don't Have a Vision and a Growth Strategy

An absence of a business vision and growth strategy can make you lag in achieving goals. As a woman or minority business owner, understanding where you're going and what you have to do can expand the entire business proficiency, quality, efficiency, and key measurements.

Many businesses have experienced a margin of success without any vision or plan. You may achieve great success without setting a vision or strategizing goals. Still, this approach is an exception and a costly risk in terms of money and investments without a compass. So much so, the absence of these two things can end up burning your business to the ground before it takes off. The lack of a vision also adversely impacts the outlook of employees' livelihood. For today's job market and how tribalism has affected how people socialize, being a part of a pact or team has shared values and interests. Without a vision or a cause, workers tend to feel unimportant and lack the motivation to work hard. Employees work best when they are motivated to come to work each day, engage around a vision, or elevate confidence in the company's vision and future. When employees feel a lot of ambiguity, and there is and no compass to mark direction, the future seems dubious, driving some of them away from being a part of your business. This discouraging impact of not setting a vision and a growth strategy is debilitating and threatening.

How to Define A Vision for Your Business

Your company's vision should be short and simple so that your employees can recall and recite it quickly and easily. If the vision isn't easy, it can become the reason for your goals and success to lag. The people who signed up to be a part of your team are essential to helping you reach the summit, and having a clear understanding of the vision is the secret sauce. Take a look at some famous vision statements.

- **Microsoft**: (at its founding): A computer on every desk and in every home

- **LinkedIn**: Create economic opportunity for every member of the global workforce.

- **Disney**: To entertain, inform, and inspire people worldwide through the power of unparalleled storytelling, reflecting the iconic brands, creative minds, and innovative technologies that make ours the world's premier entertainment company.

A fun way to create a vision for your small business is to invite your key staff members and a few front-line employees to a vision session where you brainstorm, share ideas, and list them on flipchart paper around the room. You can share and ask thought-provoking questions about your business's direction and where everyone sees the company in 3-5-10 years into the future.

> *"And the Lord answered me, and said, Write the vision, and make it plain upon tables, that he may run that readeth it."*
> **-Habakkuk 2:2 King James Version**

As a leader and the owner of your small business, ask yourself a couple of questions. "What do you want to achieve? What do you want your business to become in the future? Link "what you want" with "what you have to do" to achieve it, and you will see your vision come alive before your eyes. Know that a vision is sort of a plan for your business's future. Do not confuse it with an outline of the company's purpose and day-to-day operations. When you believe in your vision, it becomes your destiny.

The vision for your small business must have two of the following components.

1- Core Beliefs

Your business's core beliefs are the secret sauce that motivates your leaders and the employees to love what they do. It impacts the workplace and the customers to a great extent. Your core beliefs drive business performance and the ideals that create excitement and energy. Simply put, your company's core belief is the identity of your business, which keeps it centered in an ever-changing marketplace. The evolving technologies or new fads shouldn't affect your company's identity and core beliefs. They should always make you keep your eyes on the prize and keep your team-centered. When you look back at the path that brought you to the present, it should remind you why you are committed to your vision. To keep your business growing and to move forward, make sure that your core beliefs remain constant in an ever-changing business world.

2- Imagining Your Future

Imagining your future is what and how you want to see your business in 10, 20, and 30 years. Your company's future should be powerful, vivid, and meaningful so that your employees can find the drive in themselves to achieve that future wholeheartedly. The future that you aspire to achieve may seem unattainable now, but you have to muster up the courage and strength to keep moving forward and towards your dream, no matter what.

How Do You Create a Plan to Achieve the Vision?

Running a business isn't as simple as one considers it to be. Every day presents a different challenge than business owners and entrepreneurs have to overcome. But how you deal with these obstacles is what matters the most. By not losing your focus and staying motivated, you learn how to push through the situations to achieve the vision you set for your business. By challenging negative thoughts, staying self-motivated, and seeking help from a mentor when needed, you can surely accomplish your vision.

Keep your eyes on the prize! Growing up in the sixties, I heard grown folk convey this expression as a song. It was one of the anthems during the Civil Rights Movements and kept the grown folk in my neighborhood motivated and uplifted. As an entrepreneur who owns a small minority business, it is anything but difficult to get diverted, lose inspiration and motivation while building your business from the ground up. You will see a wide range of examples of different business visionaries who have made their name in the world. It may make you question your plan and objectives. "Will I ever get to that level? Will my business be recognized like theirs?"

Questions like these will surely linger in your mind from time to time. Still, it is vital to understand that we, as people and consumers, always like to concentrate on the successful business leaders and the entirety of their triumphs. However, we never talk about their failures to get to where they are. Try not to let the big business visionaries cause you to stop keeping an eye on your vision.

Remember, running a business is like running a marathon. You will have to bear with your share of ups and downs, but the trick is not to get discouraged when things do not go according to plan. If you delight in the journey willingly, you will find motivation in all junctures.

The following are some ways that can help you keep your eyes on the prize and stay focused to achieve positive results.

The Journey Matters

Try not to focus on outcomes, especially early on in your business journey. Instead, assemble a plan, ideally one with a lot of small targets. Not only will such a procedure keep you focused, but it will also give you the inspiration to keep moving in the direction of your ultimate objective, i.e., your vision. By accomplishing little achievements, you will positively impact your employees and see a clear improvement in their performance. Understand that each business experience has various hiccups, yet the lessons learned are to be used to help you evolve and become a great CEO. There is no need to get frustrated when your plan goes awry, when a potential client rejects your proposal, or when your business doesn't hit the target profit margins. The best mindset that has served me well is to enjoy the journey and learn from all good and bad experiences.

Build Relationships

While running a business, you never know when you'll find yourself on a slippery slope. In such times, you will need to be able to know who has your back, who are your alliances, and who are your "steady Eddies" who are there with you for the highs and lows. Don't wait for a crisis to build these relationships. Instead, focus on building a strong association with your family, companions, clients, and colleagues. They will be your support network when things are not going well for you and help in the valley and be with you as you strive to reach the summit.

As you become successful, it is easy to become distracted by things that provide instant gratification. You might start forgetting about your vision and feel entitled to your success. When you feel your ego beginning to control your decisions, leading you to put material wealth over your business's needs, stop yourself, and do not let your ego or desires take control over you. Invest your time in minding your business and pace yourself to win the long game. Staying grounded in sound values, work ethic, and relationships that support you will give you satisfaction and lead you on the way to build a lasting business.

Do Not Let Failure Stop You

As an entrepreneur, you should always know that success is not constant, and there are times when you will fall before making your way to the top. But do not let these setbacks discourage you from achieving your vision. The key is to learn something valuable from your failures. Disappointments are the most valuable learning to develop your constitution. Everyone who is known as a successful entrepreneur today has faced them. If you acknowledge disappointment as an inevitable part of your journey, you will find it easier to encourage yourself to continue pushing forward. When you fall, get up, and improve the process until you overcome the obstacle and perfect your strategy.

As an entrepreneur, you will battle the failures by facing them and taking risks. If the risks don't pay off, consider them as a means to learn a valuable lesson. Mistakes happen all the time when you run a business but avoid fatal mistakes as best as you can. All business owners and entrepreneurs face failure, but the successful ones don't quit. When you fail, embrace it as an opportunity to grow, expect to rise from the experience, and let failure instill persistence in you, which is highly valuable for growth and success.

Companies that Followed a Vision and Scaled to be a 7-Figure Business

1- World Wide Technology

With a current net worth of $4 billion and estimated annual revenue of $12 billion, David L. Steward's company has topped 2018's Black Enterprise Top 100 list of the nation's largest black-owned businesses. He founded the company in 1990 in St Louis, Missouri, and is still its chairman today. The company's success slowly stemmed from the poverty and discrimination he grew up in as a child. He says, *"I vividly remember segregation—separate schools, sitting in the balcony at the movie theater, being barred from the public swimming pool."*

If we're talking about successful minority-owned businesses, it would be unfair not to include David L. Stewart's I.T. behemoth Worldwide Technology, which is considered one of the largest private companies in the U.S.

World Wide Technology's Mission, Vision & Values

Mission Statement: Create a profitable growth company that is also a great place to work

Vision Statement: To be the best technology solution provider in the world

Values: PASSION, ATTITUDE, TEAM PLAYER, HONESTY

2- Blavity

A recent startup named Blavity has been making waves in media since 2014, the year when it was founded. It is an American Internet media company whose name is a combination of Black and Gravity. Morgan DeBaun, the founder, says that her experience as an undergraduate inspires Blavity. While having lunch with a few of her black friends, she was hit by the idea that an ever-increasing number of black students voiced their conversations on everything from legislative issues to mainstream society, creating a sort of scholarly *dark gravity*. Because of its rapid growth, venture capital firms have invested almost $10 million in the company.

Blavity's vision statement reads, *"Our vision is to economically and creatively support Black millennials across the African diaspora, so they can pursue the work they love and change the world in the process."*

Blavity has a post-money valuation in the range of $10m to $50m as of Jul 20, 2018, according to PrivCo.

3- Peotona Capital

Peotona Capital is a South African investment company founded in 2005 by four women—three black and one white. The company now runs a successful portfolio of investments. Those investments focus not only on making profits but also on people and South Africa's development. Peotona Capital's vision is:

- Leave sustainable footprints in communities
- Contribute to the development of women in business
- Be a model for empowerment in South Africa

So, Peotone Capital is on this list as a black-owned business and an example of a different way of doing business.

Looking at these examples, it is evident that these people showed unwavering determination and perseverance to achieve the vision they had set for their businesses and to fulfill their dreams. They devised a growth strategy and stuck to it until they reached what they had set out to do. If there's one lesson to learn from these examples, your effort and focus must align with your vision. Where necessary, calibrate your plan to solve critical issues that will impact its success.

Remember, there are countless entrepreneurs, all of whom face the same obstacles as you. Learn from your experiences and grow your circle of power in the process. By building a solid foundation of systems, relationships, and concrete goals, you will be well on your way to a successful career. Stay positive. Always appreciate yourself.

"Everybody has something in life they want.

When you put your eyes on something, you want it feels like no one can stop you.

When you finally get the prize you've always wanted, it makes you want to enjoy every bit of it.

When your eyes are focused on that prize, it makes you more determined to get it.

It almost feels like opening up a gift and seeing the one thing you've always wanted or worked so hard to achieve.

Sometimes people will try to sidetrack you if you allow them.

*You might feel like it's not easy to do, but as long as you keep your eyes on the prize, you can accomplish your goal."-***Bryson Garrett**

CHAPTER 4
YOUR PRODUCT OR SERVICE

Value Proposition

Many products and services are viewed as commodities in today's market, making them necessary for small businesses to add value to their product or service from the very start. The value of a product or service is based on two principles: how a product or service fills a need and why it is better than your competitor's in the market or industry. There is no doubt that the lack of value in any product or service can drive a business to its failure. The thing is, when you are selling products and services with no defined value, you can never use the cost points or profit margins to forecast a promise of long-term growth and profitability.

How you set your cost and price can significantly impact your business. Know that your set prices do *not* always need to maximize your margins. We, as entrepreneurs, need to understand the effect of pricing. It has a significant impact on our businesses and helps us choose better and effective pricing strategies in the future. Tons of small companies use pricing to change market share, compete in the market, or create different revenue channels.

During one of my coaching sessions, a client came forward with his problem. He seemed exasperated and fidgety with his pricing for products and services. I asked him a straightforward question, "If you are frustrated with your margins and your costs are increasing, what is stopping you from taking a look at whether your products and services are priced competitively?"

You see, pricing products or services for small businesses is a challenge, and it is not uncommon that the small business owners do not take an in-depth look at all of the elements related to what they are selling. For business owners, pricing is either the magic or doom of profit margins. In my client's case, he had been in business for more than fifteen years as an exhibit company specializing in tradeshow setups, installations, and showroom exhibits. Ten years ago, he set his price points for setups, labor, and teardowns. Since then, the setups and installations have become more sophisticated, customized, interactive, and labor-intensive. He had to contract an IT professional for some of those setups to do the networking interface. My client was frustrated because all the industry changes ate away his profit margins, and he had to cut corners by reducing his employees' pay, causing many of them to quit or work for his competitors. It also caused him to hire temporary workers who lacked expertise. This shift massively impacted customer service and customer retention.

This domino of events happened because he did not do a cost analysis and pricing to be competitive in his industry. He feared that he would lose customers if he increased his price points. Ironically, he lost many of them anyway.

Pricing, Profit Margin, and Sales Volume

The value you set for your products and services is a success secret, as it will determine your sales and revenue. Pricing and determining your cost point area involves little science, a little math, and a little research. If you get this right, your reward is a higher return for your effort *if* you don't lose sales. On the other hand, higher pricing that brings down sales volume can diminish or deplete your return because your overhead expenses per unit continue to increase as you sell fewer units. Similarly, the impact of price on sales volume is sometimes a source of stress and angst for business owners. One of the most evident influences that pricing will have on your business is an expansion or contraction in sales volume. Expanding your cost may bring down your sales volume, somewhat helping you compensate for decreased volume with higher (total) returns produced by higher margins. Bringing down your cost can expand your profit if your sales jump, diminishing your overhead cost per unit. Again, for that, you will need a little science, a little math, and a little research. So, test the market's reaction to cost increments by changing costs in focused/targeted territories before implementing the cost increment across the board.

Business Positioning, Market Share, and Competition

The value/price you set for your products makes an impression on certain buyers about your business, building an apparent and perceived worth. Value influences your image, brand, or position in the market. Simply put, high prices can tell the purchaser that you have high-quality services, or else why would you be charging such costs? Then certain customers search for low-priced items, thinking they'll get the quality they need at a lower price. Putting your products and services on sale can give out the impression that you can't sell them at your standard cost, or you are merely telling the buyers that they have an opportunity to get a great deal.

Your product or service value and price make you a competitive entity in the marketplace as it influences the size of your business footprint in terms of your share in the market's volume. Businesses tend to lower their costs briefly to gain market share from their competitors. After the buyers have had the opportunity to try out the competitor's product or service, and this strategy attracts and retains new customers, the competitor gradually raises their costs again to the point that won't cause the customers to leave their brand.

There are some situations where selling products or services at a lower cost is solely for gaining the market share from a potential competitor. Such tactics are called guerilla tactics, and they are applied by small and large businesses to exert dominance and control over the pricing and availability of products or services. When the costs are raised, and the customers have limited options or alternatives, the competition has been relatively eliminated. FYI - some laws govern these types of tactics.

Let's look at how you can create and build value for your products and services.

How to Create Product/Service Value?

> *"The more you focus on the value of your product or service, the less important the price becomes."*-**Brian Tracy**

The goal is that we should want our customers to *LOVE* our brand, and products, and services. We should always work toward adding value, regardless of what we sell or offer. "My product is unique. I don't need to add value to it." The truth is that no matter how unique or excellent your product is, there is always worth in measuring the value. Let's take a few things that you can follow to add value to your products and services.

1. The primary method to build value is the speed of delivery and providing the value that you promised your customers to make them feel happy to pay your price. People who are successful in their businesses have realized that consumers expect service instantly, and they will pay for service and convenience. A consumer, who didn't know that they needed your products or services until now, feels the need to have it right now. Buyers understand the relationship between speed, convenience, and the value of what you offer to them. A brand or a business that can perform quickly is viewed as a superior business or brand, providing a more significant level of value than the companies that move at a snail's pace.

2. We all know that our total offer is always much more than the products or services, but we can add more value by providing extra attention to our customers. Creating and delivering value offers makes the customer feel like a VIP, a very important person, to be a profitable business. Added value is a differentiator. Women and minority business owners need to comprehend that having our customers feel special is highly significant for setting yourself apart from your competitors. Simply put, give your customers a significant level of service, insight, and information about what you do. Convey that you want to make it easy for them to buy by learning more about their needs to help you add value to your products and services. As you know more about your customers, here are a few questions to ask yourself:

- Who are my customers?
- What do they want and need?

- What is my expertise that can help my customers?
- How can I teach my customers with my expertise?

After answering all these questions, you will start seeing a clear path to advise your clients. Doing so will enable the customers to use your product and services smoothly and without any doubts.

Always remember that if you want to deliver real value, you need to provide a higher level of advice that is more valuable than what your competitors are offering.

3. Another way of creating value is by offering far better and greater quality than your competitors and at a similar cost.

> *"Quality is whatever the customer says it is."*
> *–Anonymous*

Quality doesn't mean that you start adding many additional features to your existing products and services to gain more prominence to inflate your business falsely. Your client's particular needs define quality. Do not overwork yourself and make impulsive decisions. Conduct customer surveys to determine what your customer wants and needs. Once you know what your customers want, the next step is to deliver it faster than your competitors. Peter Drucker said, *"Quality in a service or product is not what you put into it. It is what the client or customer gets out of it."*

I suggest that all of my readers thrive with the same vision to create great value for your products and services.

4. As I mentioned earlier, there is always some room in your products and services to add more value, so keep searching for innovation and ideas to add value to all you do. Remember that your competitors and new competitors compete in the same space as you with remarkably similar offerings. A singular approach to selling your products or services becomes the least effective to gain and grow market share in such a competitive market. If you need to stand apart, think about how you need to stand out with the goal that your clients see you and perceive your worth to be better than that of your competitors. You can increase the value of a service or product with a personal message by improving the packaging or tweaking the design. You can even build its value by streamlining its strategy, simplifying it.

Let's take a great example. Apple has changed the PCs' whole universe by making them simple to use. Even an unsophisticated individual, who has never held such a device in their hand, can access and navigate its features. This kind of straightforwardness and easy access have given companies and businesses a chance to add tremendous value to their products and services.

5. Another way you can add value to your products and services is to expand the comfort of buying and utilizing. Again, the example of Apple devices says a lot about their value. One more example of easy access and comfort buying is 'fast-food eateries.' Thousands of people pay for comfort and easy access instead of taking a drive across town to get groceries, come back home, and then cook a meal. Creating value and expanding it also includes improving the customer experience. It is a well-known fact that customers are attracted to warmth and friendliness. Their decisions are influenced by how a brand or business deals with them. Train your employees to create an experience that is inviting. When consumers feel they are essential, they do not hesitate to buy. Whether large or small, all businesses will make farewell to place a premium on customer service to attract and retain customers in a quickly evolving marketplace.

6. A good exercise for tracking profits and losses is understanding your price points and overhead costs. Here are a couple of tips on evaluating if your products or services are priced competitively, regardless of if you are a startup or making millions:

Focus on the Company Brand: How does your price point impact your brand? I believe pricing your product or service conveys a story about the business. Whether you specialize in fine-dining or designing footwear, how do your consumers differentiate your offerings from your competitors? As an example, the discount airline *Ryanair* is the master at this. Their price is a clear call to the market – don't expect much because you're not paying much. They have a storyline that sells value for the price.

Focus on the Customer Experience: Remember your *why* and the problem you solve with your product or service. Secondly, how does what you are selling benefits your customers? Setting or resetting your price point, remember to describe how your product or service makes their lives better, easier, or more profitable.

Do the Analyses: Your price analysis is fundamental to determine the cost for your products and/or services and sales. Factors to think about are manufacturing, labor, distribution, and marketing. A few more things that you can think about are:

- Establishing what the customer will pay

- Determining price elasticity when there are changes in pricing is not necessarily constant. An example is how gas prices fluctuated during the coronavirus pandemic and returned to normal rates as the market recovered

- Analyzing competition

- Assessing legal and ethical constraints

Providing a Unique Selling Proposition (USP)

A USP is one of the principal parts of any strong marketing campaign. Essentially, it's an outline of what makes your business extraordinary and significant to your target market. It responds to one of the most critical concerns, a question that you might ask yourself a lot: *How can my business, its products, and services benefit my customers better than my competition?*

A Unique Selling Proposition, USP, is something that defines your company's *unique* position in the marketplace. A USP is considered an important aspect for creating and building a business that customers love and creating the right pricing. A strong USP will help you stand out from your competitors and actively focus your energy on creating things that would provide, offer, and deal with your ideal and targeted group of customers. It is vital to communicate to your target audience why your product is different than others, regardless of your business being B2C, B2B, or B2G. An experience of friendliness and ease for customers is a major aspect of USP. So, offer a set of benefits that will make your buyers feel like a VIP – a very important customer.

*"To be irreplaceable, one must always be different." -***Coco Chanel**

There is no doubt that communicating your business's unique selling points to your customers and instilling them into their minds is difficult, especially regarding buying. To target potential leads, developing an achievable and relatable USP is the start of the buying process. It enables your business to showcase a believable sales message and your differentiators' strong profile. Remember that a company with USP always stands for something specific and authentic. Unlike other businesses, a USP doesn't struggle to be known for several things. As an entrepreneur, you might have a dream of doing several things at one time in your business. You might want your business to be known for *everything*, but remember that you don't become known for anything when you attempt to be known for everything.

> *"Differentiation is one of the most important strategic and tactical activities in which companies must constantly engage."* **-Theodore Levitt, author, and professor at Harvard Business School**

If you want your business to stand out, build your unique selling proposition carefully, and focus on one thing rather than a lot of things. Ask yourself again and again, "What is it that your business and products have that your competitors don't?" Most businesses and companies do this one thing wrong. They try to be the best instead of being different, making them lose their market position. For instance, if you own a restaurant, would you want your restaurant to be called the best one in your town or the one everyone wants to go to because it is *the* place?

If small business owners start creating their USP effectively, the competition will become a mere name in a dictionary. It won't mean anything to you when you simply change the game rules that every business has played throughout history. For years, people have been taking cabs the usual way, but did we ever think that someone would bless humans with such ease and calm by innovating and offering a cab service through a phone app? What does this tell us? It tells us to provide people with something they haven't seen, heard, tried, or read before.

Observe your competitors and come up with things that could make your business unique in its way. Your USP should provide a solid foundation of what your company stands for. It should provide smooth engagement and consistency between the customer and you. Gain attention, build trust and make your place in the market by solidifying your business' motive and focus. The following are some steps with which you can begin creating your USP.

1. Comprehend the Characteristics that Customers Value

First, conceptualize your clients' value about your products and services and those of your competitors. Move past the things that seem normal to all providers in the market and take a gander at the rules that clients use to choose a service or product to purchase. By doing this, you'll improve your brand, and by differentiating attributes, you'll become recognized. Also, talk with sales reps, client support groups, and your clients.

2. Rank Yourself and Your Competitors by Criteria

Distinguish your current top rivals. By being objective, score yourself and your key competitors on a scale of 1 to 10 for each key characteristic you learned from your research. Where conceivable, base your score on purely objective information. Where this is not possible, make a valiant effort to see things from a client's point of view and afterward make your best conjecture.

3. Distinguish Your Rankings

Creating a graph of these points will help you spot your strengths and your competitors' shortcomings. After this, devise a straightforward, easily conveyed message or statement to communicate your USP. When distinguishing your USP, ensure that it's something that truly matters to your clients. There's no reason for being the best in the business for something they couldn't care less about.

4. Protect Your USP

The last thing is to ensure that you shield and protect your USP. You can be sure that your rivals will do what they can to kill it when you begin to advance a USP. For instance, if you have the best site, they'll get a superior website specialist. Then again, if you have an extraordinary new feature in your product, you'll see it in theirs one year from now.

When you successfully set up a USP, it will become necessary to protect it no matter what. Let the competitors struggle to keep up. By the time you feel them be a step closer to you, you would have proceeded to the next stage. In the end, when you've built up a USP, ensure that the market is continually thinking about it.

Role of Market Demand

Demand for a service or product is the quantity that people are willing and can buy at a given price in a given time. Another critical concept is sufficient demand. If the need for a product is proven by the willingness and an ability to pay, demand is sufficient and matters in the market. The fundamental law of demand varies inversely with the price, for which the market price makes a product or service more affordable. An increase in the price makes the product less affordable. For instance, the demand for a certain energy drink depends on the price based on the drink's quantity. If the price goes up, you will notice a decrease in demand, but you will see an increase in demand if the price goes down.

Market demand is a broad notion comprised of consumer demand for a product in an industry. To see your position, you need to keep a comprehensive market scenario in your mind. Market demand plays a vital role in framing broad marketing campaigns. To make it simpler, when the price decreases, we need to distinguish between the income effect and the substitution effect. If the price of a product goes down, the energy drink becomes cheaper in our case. That's because a fall in the price increases consumers' real purchasing power. If the price decreases, it allows people to buy more energy drinks with a given amount of income for everyday products.

Numerous individuals have mistaken customer demand for customer desire. These two ideas aren't similar at all. Customers can desire/want a product or service and may not bear the cost. In this way, they will not be able to buy it. Economic demand means quantifying the people who need to buy a service or a product and can bear to buy them at a specific cost. In simpler terms, demand quantifies the number of products and services customers are happy to purchase and ready to buy at a given price.

Remember that as the product's cost changes, so does the demand. Fewer individuals are willing and ready to buy products at more significant expenses. In this manner, demand goes down as costs increases.

Market Research

Realizing and knowing about the market demand can help educate future online business owners on which industry is generally beneficial. So, entrepreneurs should do market demand research before launching their startup. Market demand research includes going through studies, surveys, information, and general data about a sector or an industry.

This intelligence consists of a few distinct methodologies, an organized and sort-out technique for amassing figures, cautious understanding, and factual reporting. Another way to think of market intelligence is:

- Target industries' insight and their highest potential.

- Intelligence to glean a deeper understanding of your customers' challenges.

- Intelligence to provide you more confidence and relevant data when talking to customers and prospects.

- Intelligence will allow you to connect and retain your customers by staying informed on industry trends.

However, that doesn't mean that new entrepreneurs need a whole advertising and marketing office to understand the market demands.

There are three techniques they can utilize when directing market research.

1. **Reviews**: Social media platforms are magnificent places to post surveys about products, businesses, and services. Discover online what people think and state about a specific product or service. Send a study in an email, requesting that everybody forward it to more individuals. The more well-defined scope an entrepreneur utilizes, the better their statistical surveying will be. There are numerous studies and reports available online. If you decide to change your business, check the sources and investigate how the information or data was collected depending on these online reports. That's because some studies focus on a particular segment of the market, which can skew the results.

2. **Experiment**: Conducting experiments can be tedious and costly. However, it can also be helpful to an online business. For instance, offering another product at a lower cost is a decent method to determine whether customers approve of it. This tactic requires a great deal of client association and a relentless pledge to following outcomes after some time.

3. **Observe**: Simply glancing around and observing, both in the physical and digital business worlds, can give great signs about the market demand. This can involve reading publications or newspapers within a segment where entrepreneurs want to sell their product or service.

4. **Focus Groups:** Essentially conduct discussions guided by a set of questions to gather feedback and input based on the interaction between group participants and the research consultant. Focus groups are very popular to collect qualitative data from target consumers.

How to Leverage the Demand?

Once you have researched and studied the current market demand, you need to learn how to utilize that information for your business's benefit. Introducing a new product or service can be lucrative, especially if the market research indicates a need. When you submit a product or service in demand and market it well, you'll have the edge over your competitors. Here are some ways to leverage market demand to your benefit.

- One approach to leverage market demand is to offer a product or service that the market values. Researching products and services is the standard procedure most organizations employ to create or upgrade their products and services on the market. For retail organizations, this implies taking surveys from the target audience, collecting client reviews, sharing them with the business owners, and informing them about the kind of products or services they should create or improve existing ones.

- Sometimes, creating a demand for your products and services becomes important, especially when you already have a unique service or product to offer. If you want your product or service to run its course like a true king in the market, you need to create circumstances where people start demanding your product even before it has come out (putting up ads/offering pre-orders). This way, you will have the market following your product, rather than you following the market.

- Promotions are a common and regular business function utilized to drive organization or product demand. It is a marketing component where you pay for publicity and uses media to inform potential customers about a product, service, or organization. Conversations: dialog with buyers to influence them or increase sales) that attracts potential clients. Effective promotions can turn the market demand toward your product, highlighting your product or service's benefits over the contending alternatives (competitors and their products).

- In case you're a startup and a small business owner, your business ought to introduce its new product or service and demonstrate that it can take care of the issues your customers are facing. You can do that with the help of informative and educational content. Define your target demographics and research to find out how to approach them. Find out where they are active on social media and then inform them about your products' value.

- Coming up with an extraordinary product or service has its share of benefits, but it can present significant difficulties too. A unique perspective or idea that can bring you great success can also become an obstruction. A one-of-a-kind product or service needs to develop trust with the target audience and create a need. Luckily, there are numerous ways you can use to build trust with your customers. A marketing mix that uses the most suitable techniques for your product can help you create an appeal in the market.

- Scarcity tips the supply and demand scale in your favor and creates a sense of urgency in consumers' minds. If done right, scarcity can push a prospective customer to purchase your products. Since you will be bringing a unique product to the market, you will have novelty on your side.

- Depending on the kind of product you offer, you might have the option to utilize exclusivity as a device to create demand. When your product or service is exclusive, it means it is only for a select few clients that you have targeted based on specific criteria. The additional advantage of making your product exclusive is that you decrease or altogether dispense your competition. Basically, by introducing exclusivity, you are offering the idea that your products vary from some others on the market currently. This technique is typically best held for a high-end product line that can use premium branding. Brand names and patents can likewise help build exclusivity for a product.

How to Use Brand, Reputation, and Relationships to Your Advantage

One of the most significant parts of an effective business is branding. It's what makes you stand out among your competitors. Your business's image is an immediate impression of what your clients ought to anticipate from you. Your business image is comprised of your voice, your purpose, your promotions, your website, and your packaging. It becomes the basis on which the individuals pick you over the other brands. Branding isn't only a logo. It's imperative for small businesses to create such a brand that helps them welcome steadfast and loyal clients.

It tends to be challenging to get your first set of customers and clients when you have just started your business. So, to begin bringing in the revenue, it's smart to look for the "low-hanging fruit" and take advantage of whatever opportunity you can get. There may be times when you charge less than what your products or services are worth just to gain traction in your business. But with a strong brand footprint, you will appear to be an expert in the coming years, and then you will be able to charge like a big brand. If you prove that you produce quality services or products, customers will be bound to value what you offer and will willingly pay greater prices for it.

Effective branding is the key to building recognition and faithfulness in your business. Clients are attracted by brands that they find relatable. Connect with your customers and see if your brand is gaining your desired position. Your brand's value should always be shown through your brand and have an emotional connection between you and your customers. Create a brand on such grounds that its image impacts your customers, and they start referring you to other similar brands.

Brand loyalty is the single most crucial aspect of a business. Thus, the importance of building new relationships and maintaining the existing ones cannot be undermined. After all, this is what creates long-lasting brand loyalty. Now, to build new relationships and connections in business and maintain the existing ones, you will have to establish a reputation for your brand. Several factors come into play when you wish to create your brand's reputation to develop lucrative connections and build a loyal customer base. Some of those are:

1. Distinguish who your optimal client/target audience is.
2. Secure your online presence.
3. Give essential and valuable information.
4. Execute a review and audit tunnel.
5. Screen/monitor and react authentically.
6. Be social.
7. Value your clients.
8. Influence social media.
9. Request and reward referrals.
10. Record your frameworks.

Incorporating these components will add value to your business. The relationship you have with your customers usually begins before they turn into your clients. It only flourishes when the deal between you and the customer is made. Create such connections that make you more than a provider to them, and you will see them becoming more than a customer to you. Build your relationship on more than the deal/sales, and it'll become more than just about purchasing and the prices.

When you're attempting to create associations with individuals from your locale, keep in mind the following three things.

1. **Be Happy to Respond**. Know that there is give-and-take in all connections. If you aren't happy to be there for somebody who has been there for you, that individual will be more averse to help you when you need their help the most.

2. **It's Not Always about the Advantages**. Try not to be so centered on the ultimate objective when creating relationships. Focusing on reaching your revenue or monthly sales will force you to overlook the fact that sometimes you won't benefit from relationships and connections. Remember that your business connections won't always make you money or bring activity.

3. **Be Authentic**. Treat others as you need to be treated and welcome discussions, inputs, and new thoughts. You'll make new companions and possibly get new clients by being your true self.

*"It takes 20 years to build a reputation and only five minutes to ruin it. If you think about that, you will do things differently." -***Warren Buffett**

Reputation is essential for a business's prosperity. If your company establishes a bad reputation, it can deteriorate its prospects. An effective strategy to maintain your business's standing in the customers' eyes is by conveying the brand's message authentically and aesthetically to strengthen it further. Reputation is perceived as one of the essential components of building up client devotion and loyalty. Thus, as small business owners start basing their business on loyal relationships and customers, their aim changes from creating big sales to shielding their reputation by providing their target audience the product or service they expect.

While reputation has been perceived as a significant resource that gives a competitive edge to businesses, the businesses' administration/management needs to maintain it without fail. If you need a strong customer base, you need more potential customers to want the product or service you offer. For that, you need a reputation that stands out. Good reputation benefits business since it:

- Distinguishes your business from competitors.
- Attracts supporters.
- Builds strength to deal with non-supporters and rivals.
- Creates opportunities for development and progress.

Understand that creating a good reputation isn't just about making your business look great. It's tied to guaranteeing that your company makes its place in the more significant business eco-system and keeps developing. So, pay attention to your reputation and maintain it to benefit your business.

All of these things combined can make your business an authentic one. Do not forget to research the market, introduce your products according to the customers' needs and desires and customers' needs and desires, market demand, and maintain relationships with your customers to ensure your business's great future.

CHAPTER 5
MANAGED GROWTH

At a fundamental level, growth refers to the organization, the leaders, and individuals. When a business reaches a point where expansion and growth seem necessary to create more profit, it is called business growth. It is one of the most critical functions of a business and is carried out when big or small companies require or desire equity value creation.

According to the Census Bureau, the U.S. is home to roughly 2.5 million black-owned businesses. However, the majority are sole proprietorships or micro-sized companies, an increasing number desire to grow regionally or nationally. Most small entrepreneurs and business visionaries initiate and maintain a business, expecting to expand it at some point in their lives. In contrast, others have no desire to do so at all. When accomplishing a specific degree of achievement in their business, most small business owners and entrepreneurs are happy and satisfied to remain at the same level throughout their lives. They feel safe inside that space, and their business continues to revolve in the same market. They have little to no inspiration for transformation, growth, or progress. When small companies ignore growth and progress, they become a hazard.

We need to understand that growth isn't only significant for an organization, but it's also substantial for each employee. Without development and growth, activities, operations, functions, revenues, and profits are bound to deteriorate, bringing about low value for services or products, diminishing client support and employee confidence, and creating a large set of different issues.

Let's take a look at a few different things that could work against your business if you decide to remain the status quo instead of expanding or growing your small business.

- Your earnings neither decrease nor increase.
- Your employees stop expecting more from the business.
- You are unable to create additional employment.
- Employees who seek growth and development leave your business.
- You are left behind in the industry while your competition grows rapidly.
- The potential of your employees is limited.
- A few advantages of growing your small business are:
- More noteworthy resilience or sustainability in the market for your business
- Lower costs because of economies of scale
- Market strength and dominance
- More prominent purchasing and bargaining power
- Power to moderate business dangers through enhancement
- The decrease in the competition threat
- Strength to endure downturns and fluctuations of the market
- Drawing in the best staff and talent

The best aspect of growth is that it offers your business and others the chance to mature, progress, and thrive with it. If you want to open new doors in terms of opportunities for your business and teams, it is essential to seek growth. That is the primary reason why growth is significant in any business. As business owners, we need to understand that nothing remains the same. It either gets better or terrible, and you either progress or recoil.

There's nothing wrong with running a business with no promise of growth or development, but the consequences are dire, and you need to understand the results of not growing or expanding your business at all. However, when you know the importance of growth, try not to grow just for the sake of development and progress. Grow for new possibilities, opportunities, and wealth for yourself and other people associated with your business.

Becoming complacent in your current position can act as a deterrent to your business's success. Your business would continually face the danger of being left behind by your competitors. When you decide to remain static and stay in one spot, you allow your competition to take the bigger portion of the market, including your clients. You can miss out on various opportunities when you neglect your business's development and growth. You can lose your clients and loyal employees to your competitors as a result.

Whether you're selling food supplies down the side of a road or sitting at the top of a vast organization, you should never let go of any single opportunity to grow your business and must always seek it. A growing business is a thriving business, most people believe. However, business growth brings along with it a multitude of challenges. In the case of small business owners, they discover the hard way that their decision to grow may bring about issues if their business isn't prepared to deal with expansion and growth and can even end their business altogether. Indeed, small businesses on the verge of change can face difficulties, like running out of employees when excessive orders start to come in or fall short of products to meet their customers' demands. When such circumstances take place, businesses struggle to operate decently.

Managing operational issues seems like a struggle during the growth stage. Let's look at some tips for driving growth in small businesses.

1. **Maintain a Management Role:** As a business owner, you need to maintain a specific role in the organization. If you don't want to do tasks for your employees, you need to step up and represent yourself as a leader. Suppose you feel that you don't have a strong team of people who cannot operate in your absence. In that case, it's an ideal opportunity to either replace existing representatives who are not producing the ROI (Return On Investment) or recruit extra workers so you may concentrate on the organization, the board, and the strategy of your business.

2. **Introduce Organizational Procedures and Systems:** When small business owners initiate their businesses first, they have a significant amount of time overseeing every little detail. They spend time correcting their employees' mistakes or keeping a check on products and services before they reach a customer. But when they decide to grow and scale-up, they forget that all of this won't be possible in the later events. They simply won't

have time for all this. That is why a business should have specific procedures and systems to oversee everything you used to do previously, like managing staff and checking on quality and control of the products and services. To drive growth in a better way, make sure that your business relies on procedures and systems.

3. **Main and Check Your Growth:** With rapid growth comes rapid change. You will start generating more sales than you ever had before, resulting in more money spent than before. There might be a need to upgrade a few things and add individual items to your system. Hiring more people could also be on your mind. With all these things coming at you like bullets, it is customary to get overwhelmed, but it is at this time that you need to keep a strict and proper check on your growth. While all the additions and upgrades might seem excellent for your business and its income, being too complacent can result in damaging your financial stability. If you don't want your profits to decrease and turn into a cash flow problem, you need to keep growth in check.

Tips to Manage Your Business Growth

Your business is like a child that needs a lot of support. You need to nurture it and help it become strong and healthy, so negligence toward growth isn't favorable. Many great organizations and business owners have fallen into that trap and fizzled subsequently. If you're sufficiently blessed to have discovered success with your small business, you still need to seek the opportunities to grow and expand your business, but before doing that, you need to know a few aspects of growth.

1. First, you need to realize the need and time for growth. Know that planning for business growth includes a steady reassessment of every single operational part of your business. You can develop your business when the market demographics, the success of products or services, and financial stability show that you are prepared. However, these aspects may vary according to different industries. It's essential to recognize what you need to accomplish with your business. Emma Wimhurst, a business advisor, says that you should express your objective in under 50 words. The plan to reach that objective should include capitalization, market research, staffing issues, and other things that you believe are relevant to your business.

2. Numerous small business owners believe that they can deal with growth without anyone else. That is not true. Understand that taking assistance from a mentor isn't going to harm you in any way. You need to force yourself to invest heavily in quality individuals you can trust and set up severe reporting in place so that you get control over what's happening. Furthermore, it is essential to know whether your business development or growth is a direct result of something you're doing well or being lifted by a rising market. Growth can conceal significant issues. You may lack competition, have a mediocre service or product profiting from an incredible group of sales, or depend a lot on a single purchaser. Analyze your growth and keep an eye on the steps you take.

3. As your business progresses, you have to use the advantages of uniqueness and quality. You must capitalize on whatever elements make your business stand apart from your competitors

while recognizing your target group and their needs. Tempt your target audience with such marketing campaigns that are benefit-oriented with exceptional offers, services, and events that feature your business's qualities and associate the client to your brand in great ways. Furthermore, data and analytics will become your guide. Utilizing data and business analytics tools can help you gain further insight into your business strengths and weaknesses, which can be used to make data-driven marketing and sales decisions. It's important to document useful data findings and test your muscles because they may change as your business grows further. Focusing on what you believe you excel in heightens your sense of self-satisfaction, which increases your business's performance and productivity and boosts overall company morale.

4. A growth management strategy requires comprehending and analyzing your market. It is essential to research and get an idea of what your clients need and how they behave. Remember, business conditions and market criteria change continually, so study your customers regularly. It is valuable to do SWOT analysis as well, where you survey your organization's Strengths and Weaknesses and afterward distinguish Opportunities open to you and if there are any Threats you face. This will assist you in establishing a niche in the market.

5. To grow a business, you have to believe the individuals around you to get it going. Development can deteriorate if you demand controlling and overseeing every detail as an entrepreneur or administrator. Trusting your team versus managing day-to-day operations allows you to see the bigger picture to concentrate on

business development and growth opportunities. Refrain from being a leader who is absent all the time. Employees like to feel appreciated and encouraged for their endeavors, so set aside some time to engage with individuals and offer both positive and helpful criticism to them. This will cause them to feel connected with you and increase their productivity.

6. A growing business needs capital, which implies keeping a firm grasp on your income. Two of the essential things are good supplier management and stock control because you need to free up cash for growth and not have it tied up in outstanding debts or existing stock. Forecasting every week is also fundamental, so keep a check on what is coming in and what is going out of your business. New stakeholders and partners will be more prone to put resources into your organization if you have substantial cash flow credentials.

7. If you want to grow your business, know that extra capital is significant for keeping up with changing customer demands and operating everyday activities. Organizations need to keep up working funds and capital to continue developing and growing. To take in new orders, manage stock, build inventory, update your production equipment, extend your office space, and recruit extra people, a working capital financing loan is supplementary. There are a few diverse alternatives accessible in terms of acquiring a loan, so you must explore and discover loans with terms and conditions that fit your business's needs.

8. I can't stress enough how vital it is to set benchmarks, forecast your business' upcoming finances, profits, and sales, and stay

organized. You want to develop good habits now and stay consistent with them as your business continues to advance. With growth, revenue, and cash flow changes, you'll run into plenty of unforeseen costs such as broken equipment, the need to hire new employees, or an unexpected opportunity that requires you to act (i.e., spend money) quickly. It's easier to face business costs and limit the number of financial surprises if you plan.

Checklist before Scaling Your Business

Scalability is a mindset. You need to have the correct frameworks, procedures, individuals, and plans to execute it. Getting on the path to scaling your business model to keep up with your business development is critical. What might have been successful when your business was smaller might not be as effective now. For example, you may need to consider segmenting duties among new employees and redefining your business's organizational and managerial structures. Having processes for every aspect of your business, significantly change management, to modify effectiveness is essential. You must be aware of the new set of risks and opportunities presented to your company, as well as your incoming and outgoing cash flow.

Additionally, it would help if you thought big to become significant. Having a scalable business implies that you can realize your dreams, rake in boatloads of cash, and have a great time doing it. When you get your brain in the game, scalability turns out to be way simpler.

1. Recognize Milestones

To identify and recognize your business's milestones, allocating capital to each phase of your organization's growth is necessary. Start by assessing which phase will require more finances and in which stage you can run short of money. Identify the milestones and devise a plan for when you have to hit them and how. Your milestones should give you a completely planned guide for managing your business's growth and allow you to avail enough opportunities for raising money.

2. Watch for Expansion in Pre-Orders/Bookings

You'll know your business is flourishing when orders start to increase. More appointments/bookings/orders mean that you will achieve a new ARR (Average Rate of Return). According to David Skok, a five-time serial entrepreneur turned VC, to gain an increase in bookings and orders, making early access sales, guaranteeing client satisfaction, and recognizing profitable strategies and sticking with them is essential. Your ARR ought to provide you with a sure way to success.

3. Recognize Your Target Client

Recognizing your ideal client will require some investment of time. This process can push your business toward sustainable/practical growth. The first step you should take to identify the target client is to create a customer profile and describe your target demographics. It includes things like age, gender, location, and income level of your target customer to ascertain whether they can afford your offering or not. To learn and identify your target clients and audience, you need to carry out both primary and secondary market research to tell you about your customers' buying habits.

When you've recognized your ideal client, it is time for you to assemble your sales funnel. While numerous business associations adopt a vendor-driven strategy to channel a funnel plan, it is best to utilize a buyer-driven lens, says David Skok. So, before building a sales funnel, study your buyer's conduct and behavior. Take the opportunity to create a solid profile of your ideal buyer. Consider what your optimal client thinks about, how they purchase, and what kind of platforms they use to buy products and services. When you establish answers to these questions, utilize them to benefit your business.

4. Streamline for Your Buyer

When you've distinguished your optimal buyer and their needs, improve what you offer them and how you market that offering. Work out your customer profile based on significant sites and approach clients for product and service reviews. If they spend time reading blogs and other publications, try to maintain a steady supply of blogs and publications to catch their eyes. This is where Google Analytics comes into play. With the insights that these analytics offers, you can streamline your offerings to your ideal buyer's liking.

Key Points to Consider Before Scaling Your Business

If you're experiencing success as a small business owner or an entrepreneur, you must have been thinking about scaling your business. Women and minority business owners talk about it and think about growth a lot – we want to be successful and let go of bootstrapping, the hustle, grit, and grind. I would say we love the word *growth* when used regarding our business. A question like, *"is it the right opportunity to extend my business"* is also a frequent concern to take the risk or not. Well, let me tell you that scaling is hugely enticing for most small businesses. However, it very well may be nerve-wracking. Successful scaling can mean an exponential increase in benefits, yet the dangers of disappointments and failures remain intact and can forever end your business.

Let's look at some essential things to keep in mind before scaling your business.

Is It Time?

This is the first question you need to ask before scaling your business. Make sure you have considered everything. For instance, do you have an adequate understanding of scaling a business? Have you assessed whether or not, after scaling, your products and services will keep bringing you profits over the long haul? You may not have the right responses to these questions. In any case, you should have sensible and wise thoughts regarding each of these and many more questions to make the right decision for your business.

Besides these questions, ask yourself if this is what you truly need for your business. In case you're giving quality services and products to your clients, or you're content with your profits, perhaps it's not the correct time to scale. If you scale up fast, you may end up giving all that you liked about your business in the end. When you see yourself being overwhelmed by excessive orders and you can't seem to handle your inventory, you should start thinking about expanding. Still, even then, you should take some time to consider the idea of scaling. Don't jump at the very first opportunity that comes trotting your way. Take time, observe your business position, and then make a decision.

How's Your Team?

Before you plan to scale your business, assess your team and key positions. As harsh as it may sound, if you are trying to get to the summit and have key leaders who have never been there, it will be hard for them to take you where they have never been.

Scaling your business means you can handle an increase in sales, work, or output in a cost-effective, reasonable manner, AND your company can handle growth without an adverse impact on talent retention, productivity, and demand. Having the absolute best talent is imperative to scale successfully. Scaling will require devoted leaders and teams working for you who can manage the hills and valleys that will come on the way to the summit. Despite their outstanding abilities and skills, they don't concentrate solely on hiring new people. Understand that the people's talent and experience, but make sure they are a great fit with your "A-grade players" and think creatively, which will be needed to overcome obstacles and play an integral part in your business's future.

Even if you have the right kind of services, products, and approach, your progress and growth trajectory will struggle and stagnate without the best-talented employees. The most significant part of hiring is selecting and retaining your top talent and capabilities. As you scale, it is your mission to make sure your leaders and players mirror your organization's vision and mission and should be able to keep pace with the practices and beliefs that are your business's culture.

Having poor performers and recruiting people who don't fit in with your work culture could prompt bad performances and adversely affect job satisfaction and contentment of existing employees. Employ individuals with whom you can coexist and are eager about your business and what you're attempting to do. The progress of your business requires that you recruit extra staff. So take some time and hire smartly.

Furthermore, consider the individuals you, as of now, have. Observe and see if they've exhibited the abilities and potential to take on greater responsibilities with their current ones. If that's the case, offer them greater responsibilities.

What's in the Backup?

Scaling a business takes much more than having a talented team of leaders and team players. You need cash flow to maintain the operations, to retain your best talent, and the funds to cover the cost you will incur as innumerable expenses essential for managing and scaling a business. What this suggests is that you have adequate funding and operating expenses. Also, being completely content when your profits are on the rise can be a fatal mistake if you let your ego rule your behavior and pay no heed to create a budget and reallocate cash where required. Letting your ego and behavior rule how you manage and burn through your cash could be a fatal mistake that will demise your business. Not having a plan will most probably cause them to be negligent and mismanage their finances. Understand that the quicker a business matures, the more its value increases and becomes attractive to investors and bankers for funding. Try not to put yourself at risk by undertaking opportunities that have not been vetted financially. Always remember that you need cash flow to kick-start your business growth.

If you don't have enough cash, there are ways around that as well. Some grants and loans may be a suitable alternative. Some investors may be well-matched for you and your business. Find such investors and pitch your business ideas to them. Do your research to determine what type of ventures they invest in before you jump in. It will help you decide whether this approach is a good match for you and your business.

As a last resort, some entrepreneurs have successfully got funding through crowdsourcing, which can get you the cash you need and serve as a successful marketing aspect.

Do You Have a Plan?

Before scaling your business, make sure you are clear about your target. The more you are prepared, the better equipped you'll evaluate the framework to scale. Knowing your 'WHY' is not enough. To scale, you need 'HOW's' and 'WHO's' to help you achieve that vision. Ask yourself what these frameworks are? Does each phase in the framework have an understandable and reliable work process? Are daily and critical assignments designated clearly and sensibly? Do you have a reliable business infrastructure that you use consistently? If you don't answer any of these questions, consider doing more homework to scale your business successfully. These frameworks need to be worked out if you don't want to push your business in a downward spiral while trying to scale it. If you try to go ahead without a plan, your business will decline due to complications, and it will regress instead of progress in the years to come.

All women and black-owned businesses, or most of them, struggle to get a commercial bank loan. As an alternative, most of them seek alternative funding from community banks and Community Development Financial Institutions (CDFI).

According to the Stanford Institute for Economic Policy Research (SIEPR) and Kauffman Foundation, black-owned businesses start with less money when they begin and invest money at a slower rate over the years compared with a white-owned company. More than half of the disparities are based on financial capital. The report also shows that black entrepreneurs apply for bank loans less frequently than white entrepreneurs, but this stems mainly from differences in fear of having their loan applications rejected.

President Eisenhower founded the SMALL BUSINESS ADMINISTRATION (SBA) in 1953 to assist and protect the concerns of small businesses. It was established to strengthen the nation's economy and preserve free competitive enterprise. SBA's intentions have always been to help small businesses with competing and winning in federal and private markets. In 1953, SBA initiated assistance to help Americans build and grow their businesses. More importantly, it has been a resource to help the minority-owned and women-owned businesses grow. They have been the wind beneath the wings of many women and black-owned businesses, allowing them to soar and achieve the American Dream.

SBA has backed $210 million loans to small African-American businesses across eight Southeastern states in the last fiscal year. In federal contracts, $2.3 billion were awarded to the SBA's 8(a) certified firms - small businesses that have proven economically disadvantaged. Last year, over 100,000 startups and existing entrepreneurs were counseled and trained through the extensive resource partners that the SBA works with, such as SCORE, the Small Business Development Centers, Women's Business Centers, and Veterans Business Outreach Centers. The SBA has driven entrepreneurs successfully to the website Lender Match to help connect a lender to a small business owner's specific need. They continue to reach more entrepreneurs today more than ever before.

Relevant Stories of Black-Owned Businesses World Wide Technology, Inc.

David Steward and James Kavanaugh co-founded The Maryland Heights, Mo.-based IT products and services firm in 1990. This firm enables its customers to implement the technology. With more than $11 billion in revenue at the end of 2018, the firm employs over 5,000 people.

Vista Equity Partners

Vista Equity Partners is a private equity firm specializing in financing and forwarding software, data, and technology-enabled startup businesses. It was founded by Robert Smith and Brian Sheth. Headquartered in Austin, Texas, it currently employs over 65,000 people worldwide. According to Forbes, Robert Smith was a billionaire worth over $5.5 billion in February of 2019.

Briogeo

Nancy Twine's mother died in a car accident after a three-year stint at Goldman Sachs. The tragedy pushed her to reconsider her career path. She researched the beauty industry day and night, even on the weekends. She was heavily inspired by her mother, a chemist, and developed a natural face cream. Her grandmother was another inspiration source who taught her how to make natural ingredients products. In 2014, she launched a natural hair care brand, Briogeo, which targeted its customers by their hair texture (wavy, dry, thin, or curly) rather than ethnicity. The business was profitable from the start, and revenues grew quickly to $10 million by the end of 2018. The brand was launched internationally in 2018 and is now sold on Sephora shelves worldwide. It's also available on Cult Beauty, a UK-based online beauty store. She sold a minority stake to Drunk Elephant investor VMG last year for an undisclosed sum.

Esusu

Abbey Wemimo, a Nigerian-born entrepreneur, and his business partner, Samir Goel, founded Esusu in 2019. Their mobile platform helps marginalized communities build credit, access capital, and save money. Esusu has helped renters get credit for making their monthly payments on time. It launched a fund that provided rental assistance for people affected by Covid-19 and has raised nearly $200,000. It has more than 200,000 users and expects to take its revenue to $1.2 million by the end of 2020.

Curls

Mahisha Dellinger worked in Intel after putting herself through college at California State University, Sacramento. That's when she started spending weekends working on her idea of creating a natural hair care line. Mahisha bootstrapped the business by launching it in 2002 and soon got her big break when she partnered up with Target. Today, she has her products in stores like Walmart, CVS, and Bed, Bath & Beyond, while the rest of her selling comes from online sales. Since 2002, she has not only initiated a business of her own. She has also written a book about her journey and a television show geared towards helping other women business owners.

McBride Sisters Collection

Robin McBride and Andrea McBride were raised in wine regions of California and New Zealand, respectively. Although they were half-sisters, it was in 1999 that they met each other for the first time. Till then, neither of them knew of the others' existence. Six years after meeting each other for the first time, they launched their wine business together. By selling nearly 100,000 cases last year, they have managed to rank in the 3% of the nation's wineries. Today, they have more than half of people of color working for them, and 90% of the staff are women.

These stories tell us that these enormous organizations' success began as small as you could ever imagine. They weren't generally the juggernauts that they are today. At a certain point, they were considered nothing but small businesses. Today, they have grown into international companies worth millions of dollars. Their stories tell us that, with gradual steps, solid plans, and a little bit of luck on our side, we can take our businesses to the point where everyone knows your brand. What made these behemoths break out of the group called *small businesses* and take charge of their contemporaries was their determination, perseverance, and the use of smart business development/growth strategies.

However, it hurts to see that out of millions of small businesses globally, only a handful of them ended up growing into large corporations. Yes, we have indeed come a long way, but we still have a lot of work to do to support women and minority-owned small businesses. The work will not be finished until every small business owner can develop as a CEO and access knowledge and growth opportunities in the private and federal markets.

CHAPTER 6
MANAGE STRESS ON THE BUSINESS

"People are disturbed not by a thing but by their perception of a thing."- **Epictetus**

Work, work, work. Work is what dominates our time.

The impact of the daily grind can harm your well-being in irreversible ways. High-pressure workdays, hours of the daily commute, raising kids, insufficient rest or lack of exercise, trying to manage business and life together, making ends meet, etc., can take their toll on our minds as well as bodies. The worries of regular day-to-day life can take a toll at any time and could come in the shape of *stress*. Stress is something that every human experiences in their life in different ways. It often attacks the weakest parts of our psychology.

Many people think that pressure and stress can cause them to perform better in life, but research says otherwise. Stress makes an individual commit more errors and make mistakes while having drastically adverse effects on their well-being. A study conducted by neuroscientists in the year 2013 found that even a mild level of stress can impair our ability to control our emotions. Lead author Candace Raio, Ph.D., said that their results suggested mild stress encountered in daily life, which may damage the ability to use cognitive techniques known to control fear and anxiety. According to the American Heart Association, stress causes high blood pressure, stomach ulcer, and irritable bowel syndrome. It affects our physical health because we indulge (knowingly or unknowingly) in unhealthy behaviors when we are stressed. You may see yourself reaching out to drinking, smoking, overeating, or not eating at all. All of this can have a long-term effect on your physical health.

Stress not only ruins your mental and physical health, but it can also affect your relationships. You may need to manage and fight not to let stress erode your relationships because when you are stressed, you are bound to have a low tolerance for every little thing. You may even be annoyed and miserable in a manner that has nothing to do with people and their actions. At the same time, it could impact them just because they are around you or simply connected to you as workers or family members. How you treat your family, friends, co-workers, or situations around you can be affected by your stress response. If you are continually mean to the individuals in your life due to stress, in the end, they will pull away from you. Many of them will suffer, and you won't have a decent personal or professional life.

In a world like ours, where everything is fast-paced, and everyone struggles to make ends meet, it is easy to get stressed out. You can get stressed by simply thinking about attending a meeting at the office or cooking a meal for dinner. The smallest things can make you lose your mind, but the biggest problem with stressing about the smallest things is that you never know when they become so big that they start overpowering other parts of your life. If not taken care of, it can make you lose sight of what's important and cause you ongoing depression or anxiety.

The Stress of Running a Business

Stress is somewhat mandatory for most CEOs. It's something that comes with building a business and staying ahead of your competitors. When stress accumulates, business owners *have to* discover approaches to manage it to ensure they and their workers do not burnout. Consequently, you simply cannot escape the stress that comes with owning and running a business that could surely keep you up at night.

Stress in the business world typically manifests among business owners, workers, and employees. When leaders and workers routinely work long hours, job satisfaction changes. Disengagement and a lack of appreciation often lead to marginal results, low sales, or low employee morale. A noticeable level of disengagement occurs, along with the signs of work-related stress. While stress can't be eradicated from a business workforce, high-stress levels could be dangerous to businesses' overall performance.

When you run a business, there may be days when your mind is bombarded with a high level of stress, draining you of energy and making you feel like you are about to boil over like a pot of rice. The weight of managing and growing creates pressure, which makes you think about every possible outcome, good or bad. Every entrepreneur has felt the stress of running a business in one way or another. For a few, stress is a feeling that they experience daily, particularly when things aren't going just as they like. And it most certainly doesn't vanish mysteriously once your business takes off. Business people who run multimillion-dollar companies confess that the feeling of anxiety and stress increases with the business's size, but there is another common thing that they admit to having – that is the love for their business. Despite all the stress of running a business, they love what they do and could never consider doing something other than that. The difference between you and them is the amount of time they put into managing and channeling their stress into growth.

Let's see what stress can do to your business if not managed properly.

1- Productivity

The most vital aspect of any business is productivity. If your stressors have been keeping you up at night, you will start losing focus due to feeling sluggish and fatigue. You will struggle to work efficiently and effectively, which won't be good for your business. As a result of your stress, you may respond to situations in a non-effective way, i.e., losing deals, clients, or even employees while missing deadlines, not being able to turn lead into sales, etc. You may blow up at the smallest provocations and say or do something you later regret.

Furthermore, the stress won't help you focus on the tasks that need to be done with due diligence. Under pressure and lack of rest, you are likely to make errors that will probably impact you, your business, and your customers who need you to solve their problems. The same goes for the people working with you.

As a business owner, you need to be mindful and observe your employees' behaviors. If your business, despite your high energy and great vision, lacks productivity, it is time to talk to your employees and understand if they are dealing with abnormal stress levels.

2- Time Management

Staggering and overwhelming workload, absence of support from peers, or a large number of demands at once all can add up to a feeling of disappointment and frustration, especially where there isn't sufficient time to meet deadlines. These conditions can routinely require extra time from you or your employees to continually take work home. It can result in feeling the pressure of not managing time effectively. It can also fuel you with feeling disillusioned and sometimes angry toward your business while impacting your employees' loyalty and commitment.

When you see chaos going around due to lack of managed time, take a pause, and give yourself and your employees a break. Start observing your behaviors while resetting a plan to get things done and bringing order to the work. Get into a habit of keeping a sense of order, starting from your work office. Put them into their respective places, assigning doable work to employees, saying no to excessive orders, making deals that can be done quickly, etc.

3- Employee Turnover

Stress can result in high employee turnover. It is a fact that employees tend to leave an organization where they feel dissatisfied, be it because of the environment or the lack of support from the superiors. It may not be you who is facing work-related stress but your employees, and if you fail to address the stress amongst your people, you could start dealing with high employee turnover.

As a CEO and a business owner, it is not uncommon to feel like giving up on your businesses at times. But that is the time when you need to step up and remind yourself of your vision behind the business. Treat yourself and your employees' stress so that they feel connected to you and work with you to make it better for your business's benefit instead of leaving you feeling conflicted by the needs of the company and the needs of your employees.

4- Environment

Entrepreneurs should re-examine and re-evaluate employee workload to decide if the burden is excessively demanding or something else is not working. Not addressing possible environmental issues like bullying or harassment and not taking strict action against them can cause harm your business's growth. If you do not get to the root cause of your organization's stress, you can never bring it to an end for your business's benefit.

Not noticing that a few, if not all, of your employees experience a significant stress level can lead you to ignorance. If you never observe your growing business environment, you can never determine health and stress management programs for workers to help them and your business. It could help build inspiration and ease stress not only for the employees but also for owners. Remember that happy employees/employers make a business successful.

5- Motivation

As a business owner, feeling inspired and motivated is necessary to inspire and motivate your employees. If you stay under a cloud of stress, you will lose motivation. Take control to make things work, and deal with issues without being concerned about your team's dissatisfaction. Losing motivation under stress is the worst thing that can happen. First, exercise and ensure that you always have something to wake up and show up for each day. Then ensure that your employees are not affected by your stress and lack of motivation. As a business owner, always remember that you act as a mirror for your people. They seek your attention and follow you. If you focus on demotivating behaviors, they dominate your mind and won't work for your business's success.

Growth Leading to Friction

We all can agree that running a business has its ups and downs, from which you can't get away, especially when you are growing your business. Indeed, developing organizations face a variety of difficulties. When a business grows, various opportunities and problems demand effective solutions, making you realize that what used to work a year ago may currently not be the best methodology for your business. You learn that overcoming the obstacles is essential if you want your business to grow and flourish, provided that the steps you take today don't create problems in the future.

The following are some of the common problems your business may face in its growing stages.

1- Vision and Reality

The clash between your plan and reality can happen anytime during your business's growth. You may see that the vision that appeared good for your company a year ago isn't working for you now because economic situations change. There may come times when you have to update your strategies and plans frequently. As your business develops, your vision/plan and strategy need to change to suit your business's changing needs.

Your plan to win and acquire new clients would probably change to building beneficial and profitable connections/relationships while maximizing growth with existing clients. Existing business customers, connections/relationships have more potential for profit and can provide stable income. The new relationships may bring turnover, but the profit margins and net revenues might be lower, which may not be favorable.

2- Cash Flow

Having a great cash flow is significant for any business. It's crucial for a developing business because cash constraints can be the most significant factor limiting growth. Utilizing your finances in the best way ought to be a key component in evaluating new opportunities and business planning. With restricted assets and resources, you may need to leave behind promising opportunities, especially if going after them means keeping your core business away from essential funding.

Businesses that experience upfront costs and business models that work on longer billing cycles may see cash flow scarcity in their growing phase due to the daily operating expenses. Each working capital component should be controlled to maximize and expand your free cash flow. Tight control of overdue debts and successful credit management become essential in such times.

3- Keeping Up with Market

Business conditions and market change constantly, so your statistical surveying/market research should be done frequently. Else you risk settling on business choices dependent on obsolete data, which can prompt failure in business.

You need to understand that the market is brimming with qualified competitors rising day by day. Your organization should know about your clients' inclinations and issues since they are critical to your business's success. Understanding their needs and improving their satisfaction level do impact business growth. Not utilizing the incredible market research tool can restrict your business to lag. In contrast, others lift their performance by doing their market research timely and adequately, successfully managing to stay away from potential dangers.

Not carrying out proper market research can restrict you from comprehending market demands and requests, perceiving business opportunities, planning the ideal marketing campaign, limiting misfortunes or losses, and monitoring the competitors' activities. Doing market research before growing your business would allow your business to classify goals and objectives. It would also help measure current trends and take advantage of reaching out to your target audience.

4- Balancing Work and Life

Going from having a small business to growing and expanding it to something larger can have you entangled in time-consuming things. You may feel what is called burnout. It usually occurs when excessive pressure is put on a person, which results in chronic stress. The primary reason you might be suffering from that could be the lack of work-life balance.

A growing business requires attention and significant time and effort. It could divert your attention from your personal life while forcing you to spend more time working instead of spending time with your family. Yes, staying in the office for long hours may increase your productivity but won't help your mental health. Many entrepreneurs and business owners give up or slow down their growth because of not handling the work-life balance. They feel burned out all the time, which sucks all their energy and enthusiasm, leading their businesses to fail.

There are tons of other things that your growth can lead to friction. Growing businesses often meet with different and complex issues they may have never dealt with before. All of these and many more aspects can combine and overwhelm you to the core and have you on the edge of 'I can't do this anymore.'

Wanting to Resign your Vision

The journey of entrepreneurship is fascinating. There come times when the difficulties appear to be overpowering, where some business owners are compelled to consider quitting. Particularly after facing and struggling with a few failures and setbacks in business, they start to question whether they have *it* in them to push their business to the top. Suddenly, the ground-breaking vision or plan doesn't seem practical enough to take it to the top. Self-doubt sticks to their hearts and minds while despondency starts to dominate.

Indeed, even on the best of days, maintaining a business can be unimaginably upsetting, overpowering, and debilitating. Feelings like these are natural. There will be times when you wonder if it's extraordinarily justified or worth it to fight for the business because of the burden and all the trouble. You may think about abandoning your business and seek a *suitable* job. Well, you are not alone. Many entrepreneurs and business owners have felt this, and you must not fear because thoughts like these imply that your human side is awake. As humans, we have a restricted capacity to bear things you can't control. That is truly where the pressure and stress of being an entrepreneur resides. We stress how quickly we find new clients, manage our cash flow, make payrolls, and a thousand different things. Of course, we can invest our energy in making these things profitable for ourselves, but we can't control market changes or consumer demands. That is why we often decide to resign 'our dream and vision.'

Growing and developing your business alone can feel discouraging, knock you off your game, and make you question whether you ought to abandon your business or make you ponder if accomplishing your dream and vision is even conceivable. The truth is, what you may be feeling has been experienced by many entrepreneurs. This stress makes you question your choice to initiate and start a business and your ability to run it.

Jessica Bruder, an American journalist in *The Psychological Price of Entrepreneurship*, writes about being an entrepreneur. She says that before entrepreneurs made it big, they struggled through moments of near-debilitating anxiety and despair–times when it seemed everything might crumble. There's no magic potion that you can drink to fix or manage pressure, and you unquestionably can't eliminate it entirely, but you *can* figure out how to deal with it to the point that it doesn't scare you or force you to minimize your goals and dreams.

Steve Jobs once said he is convinced that about half of what separates the successful entrepreneurs from the non-successful ones is pure perseverance. So, if you can't get rid of the stress entirely and face the obstacles while maintaining perseverance, you might use this *friction* to your benefit by focusing on having a positive mindset.

Shifting from Negative to Positive Mindset

If you want to become a successful entrepreneur, know that stress will be your constant partner on the whole journey. Indeed, stress is a significant part of a business owner's life and, at times, requires you to sleep with one eye open. No matter how constant its presence is, if you are not capable enough to handle it well, it could ruin the present as well as the future of your business. Unless you manage stress, it is easy to see yourself finding the worst in every situation, and the worst possible scenarios will locate and find you! I liken this to having a dark cloud over your head.

It is fair to feel slightly affected when there are many problems, complications, and obstacles around you. Similarly, it is easier to fall into the trap of an ongoing loop of stress. But carrying that kind of pressure on your shoulders will affect your energy, thinking, productivity and eventually dragging down the overall business performance. Stress can take over your life only when you let the negative emotions and thoughts control your mind. Taking negative thoughts or feelings and turning them into positive energy could do wonders for your health and business.

Everything in our life is interconnected. It all depends on how we choose to look at things. How we perceive them depends on our state of mind. If we want to eliminate negative thoughts, we need to understand their source. Many negative emotions come from thinking small, not feeling confident, or blaming someone or something for situations in your life. What is essential for you to understand is that you can't change the outcome of any situation that you don't have control of, so it's useless to be angry about it. Instead, focus on looking for the silver lining of a bad situation and turning it into a positive. Always remember that constant negative thoughts can weigh you down, both physically and mentally.

The following ten (10) tips will help you translate negative thoughts into positive ones before they ruin your day and even your business in the long term.

1. *For negative thinking to stop, you need to possess a healthy brain.* For that, practice getting a good night's sleep so that when you

wake up early in the morning, your mind is naturally fresh, and you feel motivated to go about your day.

2. *Push negative thoughts out.* It takes about 25 seconds of dwelling on a thought for it to enter our consciousness and affect our mood. As soon as you notice negative thoughts or images entering your mind, just say, "Stop!" to yourself. You can even say it out loud, preferably if no one is around, but it is also useful when you just say it in your head. Train your brain to reject these thoughts. Stop them before they get stuck in your head.

3. *Investing a little time in meditation and exercise every day can positively kick-start your day.* It will help declutter your head, boost your dopamine and norepinephrine levels, improve your productivity and keep you motivated throughout the day.

4. *Make time for positivity.* If you surround yourself and your life with negativity, your thoughts will never be optimistic. Make time to do things that make you happy personally. A hobby, i.e., reading, sports, anything you enjoy, is a good distraction from negativity. Focus on things that promote happiness and positive thinking and let them be in charge of your emotions.

5. *Practice the 80/20 rule.* The 80/20 rule, also known as the Pareto Principle, states that 80% of outcomes result from 20% of activities. It means you have to prioritize all of your tasks from most important to the least. Doing this will help you get significant things done early instead of spending time on the insignificant or small ones, which could leave you overwhelmed and stressed.

6. *Picture something that you are happy and grateful for.* If you start feeling frustrated, sad, or pessimistic, remember something you feel good about and focus on that. Think about your successful ventures, a great many leads you once cracked, or great sales, whatever that made you believe in yourself. Recall something you are grateful for and absorb that feeling of gratitude for a few moments. Lingering on a positive memory and experience helps to settle a positive mood.

7. *Replace the negativity around you (toxic people/things).* You may have to distance yourself from negative people or negative things. People who tend to bring you down or who you suspect are taking your business down should be avoided. It's difficult to focus on the bright side when you're surrounded by negativity. Identify the positive people in your life and spend time with them regularly. Positive people love helping others. Don't be afraid to express your admiration for their emotional health because their positive energy is a beacon of hope for you and your business. By this, you will end up developing optimistic thoughts too.

8. *Unplug and decompress.* Stress and negative thoughts can take over your mind only when overwhelmed and burdened with several situations, problems, or tasks. Unplugging from all the things for a short period will help you regain the mental and physical energy required to achieve the goals.

9. *Smile often – very often*! Even though it sounds cheesy, many people don't realize that happy thoughts can be projected from your actions to your mind. Feeling good doesn't always come

from the inside. Smiling persistently activates endorphins responsible for making us feel good. They also help us lower stress levels. Smiles are powerful, free, and extremely beneficial in building a positive mindset. Positive thoughts and happiness create a positive mindset. You can't deny that a positive attitude is a key to living a healthy and satisfying life. It's time to quit the negative thinking and invite positive thoughts into your mind.

10. *Do mental aerobics.* To conquer stress and kick out the negative emotions from your mind, you need to start training your mind in such a way that, at the time of a stressful situation, it starts finding the solutions instead of wasting time worrying about it or making up the worst of the worst scenarios. Try neurofeedback to use your brain's self-regulation mechanism to improve its performance. This type of non-invasive brain training will help you see the flaws and correct them in a better way.

The mind of an entrepreneur should be, at all times, ready to tackle unexpected things such as a discrepancy in inventory, a sudden drop in sales, loss in significant investment, etc. But when all you have are negative thoughts and emotions, it will only make things worse for your business's success. Indeed, there are several things besides negative thinking that could bring your business down to the ashes of failure. It all depends on an entrepreneur's characteristics that make or break their entire business.

Let's take a look at a few characteristics that you can adopt to handle your business in a better way.

Positive Attitude

Due to the spontaneous nature of work, a positive attitude needs to remain constant in an entrepreneur's life. The capricious demands and long hours can negatively impact your personal and professional lives. If you don't want your company's progress and forward motion to be undermined, you need to stop nurturing all the negative thoughts. It does not, in any way, mean that you see obstacles, complications, or problems through rose color glasses, but it is about using your superpowers and then channelize the positive energy to tackle and respond to them by asking yourself how you can fix the situation. Focus on things that can be controlled, and stop worrying about the ones that are either out of your control or cannot be fixed.

Creative Mindset

Novel ideas and innovations catch people's attention in today's world. People demand uniqueness and rareness, which can only be developed if its owners have a creative mindset. Even if you are not from a creative industry, having an out-of-the-box mindset can make your company successful. According to Steve Jobs, creativity is just connecting things. When you ask creative people how they did something, they feel a little guilty because they didn't plan to do it. Instead, they just saw something, and it seemed obvious to them after a while. It's because they could connect experiences they've had and synthesize new things.

Ability to Learn from Failure

Failure is inevitable when you are in the business world. The utter unpredictability of taking on a new venture and then driving it to its success makes the entrepreneurs' lives seem like a constant game of luck. But learning to cope with all that can make your business successful. The ability to learn from both small and big failures is what makes an entrepreneur or business owner better every day. Failures, at the time, may seem like they are breaking the bones of your business. But you will soon see a difference in yourself when you have gone through them. You will be more experienced and better equipped to face all future failures.

Running your business can be the most exciting thing you've ever done. But it comes with its challenges, self-doubt, and worries. While all of the mentioned things are normal, learning how to go through them is the real thing that can be dealt with by driving out the negativity and cultivating positivity in your life.

Managing Business Stress with a Positive Mindset

How many times have you heard people say, "Be positive"? Probably a million times. Because there is so much negativity in our lives, we need a constant reminder to stop indulging in it. Writer Norman Vincent Peale wrote in his book *The Power of Positive Thinking*: "I certainly do not ignore or minimize the hardships and tragedies of the world, but neither do I allow them to dominate." It means we need to acknowledge the stress and negativities instead of allowing them to dominate us. Positive thinking does not mean that you start avoiding negative emotions or pretending that life is perfect. It is about accepting the fact that things have gone south. It is about adopting a growth mindset that allows you to remain calm and deal with the storm with determination.

Being a business owner and managing stress is crucial because you are the business's sole proprietor and the anchor holding the business tightly. If you fall in the ditch of stress, you will lose not only your business but also the employees who once trusted you. Let's take a look at a few ways with which you can handle and manage your business stress.

Recognize the Good Things

It is good to recognize both what's going well and what isn't. But when you focus on the things that are going right, you naturally develop a positive mindset, which eventually helps fight the stress. When you feel like you are making progress, you are working toward the goals that will make you realize that you have control over things, even those that are problematic and creating a hindrance. Focusing on not working on things may hinder your progress only if you don't deal with a positive mindset. When you see something that isn't working as you had planned it to, take a deep breath and deal with it in such a way that it doesn't affect other aspects of your business. Focus on your business's good things because it will keep your mind in the present.

Drema Dial, Ph.D., psychologist, and life coach, says that your brain tells you that you have to stay vigilant when you're stressed. Your brain then goes into hyperdrive with all the things that could be going wrong, will go wrong, might have already gone wrong, and how you fix them. Drema adds that this is one way your brain keeps you locked into familiar routines, and that is precisely why it is significant to break the cycle that keeps you chained to unhealthy coping behaviors and keeps your stress level high.

Identify Stressors

You cannot tackle your stressors if you don't even identify them. Observe your behaviors and moods throughout the day and notice what makes you cringe or gives you strain and tension. Is it a specific client? Is it the discussion of sales that stresses you out? Do you have an unidentified problem with the work of an employee? Look around yourself when dealing with crucial and insignificant things to pick out the stressors. Exercise mindfulness to gain self-awareness and try tracking or journaling when you start identifying the stressors. This way, you would know how to tackle certain things at the end of the day.

Always remember that stress springs up when you have unsolved problems stacking up in the chambers of your mind. As an entrepreneur, you must be working around the clock, adjusting, growing, and getting things done, all of which could force you to overlook major and sometimes minor issues. Once a while, taking a step back will help you identify and recognize the issues you may have missed or those that need your attention.

Mike McDonnell, an international speaker, serial entrepreneur, global brand co-owner, and podcaster, says that self-awareness is key to identifying your stressors and your employees. Once you know what stresses your people out, you can shuffle the tasks accordingly. Knowing that a particular part of the job triggers anxiety in people can help you prepare to tackle it and change your response to those stressors accordingly in the future.

Schedule

Planning and structuring are significant when you are in the business world. It helps with the stress because when you have it all planned, you do not anticipate and worry about the results. If you want to have confidence and self-efficacy to handle whatever problems come up in the future, you need to plan and structure even the tiniest of your daily tasks. If you plan things regularly, you know that something is about to fall off the grid.

As an entrepreneur, you must think that work is your life now, and no matter how much time you spend on your business, there aren't *enough* hours to get things done. Understand that it happens when you do not plan or schedule your days regularly. Breaking down tasks and goals can help you steer clear of unnecessary stress because now you have things listed down, instead of running here and there, doing all things simultaneously. Drema Dial says that a schedule allows the person to plan, anticipate, and keep life organized. I recommend that all activities go onto a program.

Dealing with problematic situations with a positive mind cannot only help you move your business forward in the right way but can also benefit you in a variety of ways. Let's take a few benefits of having a positive mindset.

Benefits of a Positive Mindset

Being human is about forming habits and routines; even Buddha once said that we are what we think. It is very important to choose a positive way of thinking and have an optimistic attitude.

A Positive Mind Attracts Positive Events

If we decide to become positive, we can make the law of attraction work in our favor - the belief that positive or negative thoughts bring positive or negative experiences into a person's life. If you make positive thinking a habitual way of seeing life and situations, imagine how many great things you can attract into your life? When you choose a positive attitude, you will start to notice a lot of positive results, even in the worst of situations, which will help you deal with them easily. Likewise, when you start observing people with a positive mindset, you will begin to create more meaningful friendships and relationships. This attitude will create a positive atmosphere around you and your employees, increasing productivity and job satisfaction.

Better First Impression

If you make positive thinking your priority, you will always exude positive energy and make a great first impression. Always remember that people are usually attracted to positive, kind, and friendly personalities. A good first impression can significantly impact the development of your future relationship, which could help you succeed in your business. When you are about to meet a new client, a customer, or simply someone connected to your business, *smile inside* and meet them with a mind that is empty of any bias and presuppositions.

Better Health

For vibrant health, positive thinking is very beneficial. Several scientific studies have shown that people with a good positive vibe are less likely to suffer from depression and get old slower than negative thinkers. In many cases, bad thoughts are the leading cause of health issues because when you are not at ease or have constant negative thoughts, you become dull and eventually fall sick. Just change your thoughts, and you will change your life. That's why taking care of our thoughts means taking care of our health.

Positive People = More Success

Positive people are more likely to be successful than negative ones. Positive people invest their time working forward, while the negative ones waste their time worrying or pointing out flaws instead of resolving anything. When you implement positive thinking into your life, you will notice that success becomes easier, and it's not as challenging and difficult as many people think. Start working instead of worrying because all the famous and successful business people have learned from their mistakes, overcome their stress, and worked hard to be where they are right now.

Overcome Stress

The leading cause of stress is worrying and negative thoughts. If we think about it further, we can understand that stress never solves problems. On the contrary, it can leave us helpless. When you find yourself indulged in negative thoughts, start shifting your focus onto better things that have happened in the past. My mantra, as silly as it may seem, is to affirm "the universe is abundant, and opportunities come to me quickly and easily." By saying this affirmation, a feeling of calm eased my mind. Understand that positive people overcome stress more easily. When you start to increase the quantity of good and positive thoughts, stress gradually leaves your life and is barely noticeable anymore.

Positive Thinking Leads to Opportunities

Positive thinking and an optimistic attitude can turn all your problems into opportunities, whereas negativity can blind your outlook. If you turn your thoughts from the negative to the positive, your eyes will be opened, and you will see the bottle as half full instead of half empty. Whenever your business faces issues, start noticing the hidden opportunities behind them. You will begin to notice solutions and understand that every problem is an opportunity to grow. All problems can be solved, and you will finally be able to see your way to the answer.

The Abundance of Good Things

Sometimes, people live their life without knowing how blessed they are. They take things for granted and forget to be thankful. Remember that you attract what you think, and you reap what you sow. So, when people live their lives complaining and mourning about little problems, they accentuate lack and risk losing the good stuff without appreciating the things they already have. On the other hand, appreciation and gratitude can bring more good things to be thankful for into your life. Be grateful for what you have and count your blessings. Do not think about the business hawks flying high in the sky. Instead, think about your small business and the customers your serve. See the positive in every situation, and you will have more good things coming your way.

Motivation

Having a high level of motivation is the same as having wings. You need wings to fly like those hawks who you look up to, right? Understand that success doesn't find you, it doesn't come to you, but you have to go out and get it, for which a positive attitude is necessary. It will boost your motivation, and you will start to achieve your goals quicker and easier. Instead of looking for external things to drive motivation, start practicing positive thinking, and you will see an internal drive toward your goals.

This is only the tip of the iceberg for positive thinking benefits. It is a truth that being optimistic and positive is the most beneficial skill you can learn in life because the world is full of challenges, especially for an entrepreneur. Having a positive mindset is necessary if you want to compete with all the business world's big lions. If you keep nurturing the negative mindset, you will burn your business to the ground. A positive mindset will not only move your business ahead to the path of success, but it will also help you with your personal growth.

CHAPTER 7

COST TO THE BOTTOM LINE

If you have reviewed an income statement, you must know it contains every detail about your business transactions. Each of these details is equally important, but the one that matters the most is the bottom line. These are the two most important lines on the company's income statement: *The Top Line* and *Bottom Line*. The top line refers to your company's gross sales and revenues, and the bottom line refers to net income on a company's income statement. When all expenses have been deducted from the revenues, the income that remains is what we call the bottom line. Yearly or quarterly, analysts and investors look into both the top and bottom lines to see its changes.

To increase the bottom line for a company, management can enact different strategies, through increasing production, raising prices, expanding product lines, lowering sales return, etc. By following all these and other strategies, you can increase the revenue or the top line, eventually boosting the bottom line. You can also increase your company's bottom line by reducing certain expenses, decreasing wages, utilizing tax benefits, using different input goods to make products, and limiting capital cost. All of these can help increase the bottom line. If your company's bottom line shows a decrease, it means the company has either encountered a surge in expenses or a dip in income.

There will come a time when you, very confidently, can say, 'Yes, I did it.' When you have met the demands – sales are coming in, revenue is posted to the bottom line, a little profit margin is earned, good cash flow is coming in - all of this will keep you relaxed and bring you peace. You let the good times roll while lying back in your CEO executive chair when suddenly a thought comes to you: *I am ready to scale my business to be a multi-million-dollar enterprise. What's next?*

Scaling Your Business and Boosting the Bottom Line

Whether you have just launched a business or are already running a thriving business, the next step is to grow and scale your company and boost your bottom line. It is easier said than done and can be extremely difficult, no matter which industry you operate in. Certainly, there are many variables to consider when you think the timing is right to scale your business.

Remember, perhaps you were drunk with energy and excitement when you first started your business and felt like you could accomplish anything. It felt euphoric. In a couple of months, the excitement started churning and tying you up in knots. You began to feel a little panic because, to bring in revenue, you had to feed the beast. You needed money and resources to put in the business to find leads to convert to sales and revenue. And so, the euphoria turned into anxiety and stress.

Stress and anxiety are usually caused by many factors that a business owner must consider before scaling their business. When thinking about scaling your business, you would first think about pursuing a certain kind of opportunity but determining how to facilitate a meaningful boost to your bottom line should also be one of your concerns. If you look closely in your circle, you will see tons of business owners struggling to grow their enterprises because there are too many aspects that need to be considered before getting the process of scaling going.

New Markets

One of the surefire ways to boost your company's bottom line is to enter a new market. New markets provide a wealth of opportunities, but joining them can be as difficult to launch your business from scratch. It may become tricky, and you may have to introduce new processes and services to cater to the new market that you have decided to consider.

One great way to tap into new markets is to expand your geographical reach. Selling goods only in one location can limit your reach, halting your scaling process before it even begins. Be prepared because expanding your reach would give rise to your competitors, which would require you to market your brand extensively. It is an effective way to scale the business but not as straightforward as it sounds. A lot of careful consideration of every aspect is needed before hopping into a new market. Then and only then you will start seeing the increase in sales that you want.

New Customers

To increase your profits, you must secure a bigger market share. By modifying and enhancing your market activities, you can attract new customers. Running campaigns for a target audience, establishing your brand, running SEO campaigns, increasing social media activity, and enhancing the quality of your backlinks all can raise your online profile and attract new customers. Consider outsourcing this effort to a specialist firm that works in your favor to allow you to work on the business's core activities. When you outsource, you directly benefit from their expertise and reclaim your valuable time.

New Venue

It is a great first step toward scaling your business in a new market to launch a new storefront. When you launch a second or third venue, you dramatically expand your company and increase profits. With much research and due diligence, you can find the right location for your venture. It will take time, but eventually, you will find the right area to work in your favor.

You may find it easier to secure the financing you need when it comes to funding. Potential investors and lenders will know if you're already operating a successful business. Your pitch will give them confidence in your business model and your abilities, which should make them more agreeable to investing.

Stress and Pressure behind Scaling the Business

Many organizations confuse growth with scaling. Growth means adding revenue at the same pace you are adding resources. Scaling means adding revenue at a much greater rate than cost. Both are easier said than done. Scaling a business refers to the phase where once an organization has reached a certain size, resources are channeled to achieving fast growth.

Because of the confusion between the two, most companies do not successfully grow in the kind of size they have achieved for their company. This conundrum often brings many challenges, requiring significant planning, staffing, funding and backers, technology, systems, and processes.

For sure, there is an intensified pressure for leaders to keep up with the changes in the business world, which often forces them to manage their growth poorly, resulting in organizational mayhem and widespread conflict. That is why several businesses end in their first five years, leaving the owners to question the business performance.

45% of entrepreneurs report being stressed compared to 42% of *other workers*, according to the Gallup Wellbeing Index. These deviations may sound small. However, according to a more recent study, approved by the UC Berkeley Institutional Review Board and published in the journal Small Business Economics, found that mental health directly or indirectly affected 72% of the entrepreneurs, including those with a personal mental health history (49%), and family mental health history among the asymptomatic entrepreneurs (23%).

Additionally, entrepreneurs were more likely to experience depression: 30% compared to 15% and 16.6% (APA), ADHD: 29% compared to 5% and 4.4% (NIMH), addiction: 12% compared to 4% and 8.4% (SAMHSA), and bipolar diagnosis: 11% compared to 1% and 4.4% (NIMH), where the first percentage is of the entrepreneurs, and the latter refers to the general public.

Similarly, in 2019, a founder-led community named We Are 3Sixty, surveyed mental health in over 270 founders. It concluded that most entrepreneurs are suffering in silence. The survey showed that 78% of founders feel their health is negatively impacted by running a business. Nearly 70% report feeling depressed, 55% say they are burnt out, 50% experience anxiety and panic attacks, and 68% say they struggle with their sleep – a symptom is often seen as a precursor to mental illness.

"We invested in you. So if you're not happy, what's the point?" This was the point the investors said to Sukpaiboon, an entrepreneur, when she confused growth with scaling that messed up her mental health, eventually driving out all the enthusiasm and inspiration from both of her personal and professional lives. When she finally decided to acknowledge her mental health and talked about it with her investors, they understood, and the investment was written off, eventually stopping her coffee brand's trade. If Sukpaiboon stopped herself from jumping into the quick growth/scaling of her brand, she would not have drained herself and her people to a point where the trading had to be put to a stop.

Most entrepreneurs ask themselves irrelevant questions before scaling their business, which eventually traps them and their people. Instead of asking, *how quickly can I look fundable?* Ask yourself:

- As a CEO or business owner, am I equipped with the right skills and abilities to scale my business?
- Do I have the technology, systems, and processes to support growth?
- Am I designing and building systems that can expand with my business?
- Do I have the right resources in place?
- Do I have the right talent in the right seats?
- Do I have a solid leadership team to motivate and engage the employees?
- Do I have a viable plan to grow resources as the business develops?
- How will I meet increased demand?

- What am I willing to give up to scale my business?
- Do I have a support system in place for my family, friends, and customers who want to see me succeed?
- Do I have investor or funding relationships to bankroll the growth?
- Am I prepared to deal with disappointment and setbacks?
- Is the organizational internal structure sound enough to withstand the stress on its systems?

Finally, you need to ask yourself if you are growing or scaling. If you want to build a successful company, you need to scale and not just grow. A basic example, when a company gains customers, it hires more people to service the customers and add revenues at the same rate it is adding more cost. In this way, the company is growing but not technically scaling. As mentioned above, scaling is all about adding revenue rapidly by adding resources at an incremental rate. To increase margin and drive consistent growth over time, companies like Google and salesforce.com quickly add customers while adding fewer additional resources.

Scaling is all about designing your organization and creating business models. It easily scales and generates consistent revenue growth while avoiding stall-points and extra cost/resources along the way. You must have a clear idea of where you want your business to be in the next 10 to 15 years. Remember that scaling a business truly begins from its ideation stage, where you list down the expectations and realities in a straightforward manner so that you know what to expect along the way. While you are in your ideation stage, it is important to look at a few common and apparent mistakes that almost every entrepreneur is bound to make if they are not prepared.

The few mistakes that you need to avoid at all costs while scaling is:

- Scaling without a foundation
- Focusing too much on marketing and selling
- Not listening to your early customers
- Hesitation to recruit employees with a better skillset
- Scaling too quickly
- Ignoring your people and culture
- Compromising your long-term business plan for short-term growth
- A wrong balance between gross revenue and profit
- Not understanding the economic drivers of your business
- Being stuck in the product road map without improvisation
- Being unable to identify and approach different kinds of customers
- Refusing to implement change management principles
- Believing that your investors will let you play your game
- Not documenting your business processes
- Scaling a business in an organic process
- Running out of resources while scaling the business
- Risking customer experience
- Focusing on too many goals at the same time

As time passes and considering the above, everything will connect, and scaling your business won't be as stressful as you might've thought. Indeed, every entrepreneur has to face various challenges along their journey. However, it's wise to take preventative measures before starting the journey so you won't feel depressed when and if something you anticipated has failed. You will scale your business with little to no trouble when you have appropriate planning, the right team members, and a mindset to advance.

"If you want something, you can have it if you are willing to pay the price. And the price means you have to work better and harder than the next guy."
-Vince Lombardi

Everything has a price. It is a universal fact that nothing comes for free. If you want a luxurious lifestyle, you need to work hard for it. When it comes to success, there is no substitute for sacrifice. You must be familiar with it, especially when you are a business owner. Remember that every successful entrepreneur had to give something to get the kind of position they are in right now. Similarly, you need to provide your newly launched or already thriving business a few things. Those things are:

Time

Have you *just* started your business? Are you stressing about the investments? Are you struggling to get funds? Well, let me break it to you that the most important investment you can make in your newly launched business is your *time*.

"Time is money," you must have heard this phrase at least once in your life. Yes, it is. Imagine giving no time to your business. What would happen to it? What happens to flowers and children if they are not given proper time and attention? Your company, new or thriving, is like your child. It is like a flower you have *just* planted in your yard. Now ask yourself, what do you want to do with it? Leave it as it is or nurture it to grow into a tree that will give you shade and life to other creatures?

Once you have decided to step into the business world with your venture, you need to start investing as much time as possible. As a business owner, you need to be on your toes, ready to show up whenever your business requires you. Why? Because you are no longer an employee working for an eight-hour shift who can go home and forget about the work. You will find yourself excited about your venture and thinking about it in your sleep and most of your waking hours - it is *you* who is the driving force behind your business's success.

Remember that time is the first thing to invest in your business, and then comes other things. If you want to have an abundance of free time in your hands *and* have a successful business, I have bad news for you: this is *not* possible. You need to give something to get something in return. In this case, it is your time you will give.

Money

Do you want to make money? I know, a silly question to ask on my part because *obviously*, you want to make money. If so, you need to understand the meaning behind this phrase; "You need to spend money to make money."

As with *time*, money is an essential investment in your business. It acts as fuel to your business, and it ebbs and flows to demand. For someone who has just started a venture, being stationary is bad news.

We all agree that entrepreneurs, by nature, are risk-takers and don't blink twice in grabbing new opportunities. Similarly, the investment of money asks for a lot of courage. But before you think about investing in your business, there are a few things that you need to understand:

- Your business' finances

- Your finances
- Your goals

Once you have a solid understanding of all three things mentioned above, you'll be in a better position to make the right calls about how much to invest in your business.

Here is Steven Smith of Even Luxury Car Care approach: "I didn't take a salary from the company for the first 3 or 4 months. Instead, I reinvested every single penny back into ads and our packaging designs to make sure we could grow as quickly as possible. After a few months of tweaking our ads for better returns, we were now getting the same income amount for a third of the price—which let us triple our ad spend on the best-performing ads and have massive success. If I had taken a salary at the start, we wouldn't have been able to learn and spend money on ads to see what worked."

I know how it feels to live on peanut and roman noodles to have the cash flow to invest in birthing your business but trust me when I say that your startup years need your dedicated investment. However, you will start seeing the results, small at first but *mighty* to take you to the summit. Hold onto your hope and the *small* steps that will turn into *big* results before you even know it.

Energy

Entrepreneurs, having to deal with tons of things at the same time daily, are often left empty. They feel exhausted and weary. If these two things are handled and allocated wisely, you can undoubtedly harness the fading energy and save your health from falling.

Learn to say *No*. Yes, I told you to *Mind Your Business*! If you want to become a successful entrepreneur, you need to think about self-preservation – put the mask on your face first to live to help another. The mistake of not having personal boundaries on how you invest your time and resources can lead to a fatal outcome.

You are the most valuable asset in your business. Feed yourself, your mind, and your body with healthy fuel to maintain a reservoir of energy. With a healthy diet and exercise routine, your brain will do its part to help you to think critically and creatively. Your business will benefit from your investment in yourself, and your business will benefit from your intelligence.

*"Invest your energy in the things you can control." -***Steve Buckley**

While investing energy is an essential aspect of scaling or growing a business, it is also imperative to identify when and if you should invest your energy. Be wise when spending your energy on someone or something because it could result in unexpected stressors, sidetracking you from your business's goals and interests.

Avoid Burnout

Let me clear out a common misconception that entrepreneurs experience burnout because of working too hard. *False.* There are tons of people who have dedicated their whole life to their business's prosperity. If you think about it, you know business owners who love to spend their time working for their company. They work all the time, yet they do not feel burdened or stressed. Ever wondered why? Because they have invested time and resources into developing their management skills. The problem isn't putting endless hours in their business; the benefit is investing in work-life balance and support systems.

Okay, so you have all the time, money, and energy to invest in your business but no idea how to manage it. What do you think will happen? Not only you but the people working with you will also start experiencing burnout.

"Management is efficiency in climbing the ladder of success; leadership determines whether the ladder is leaning against the right wall."
-Stephen Covey

How should *you* identify if you have a reliable management system? Harvard Business Review recently highlighted a study on the relationship between entrepreneurship and burnout. According to the review, there are two types of passion. The first type is called *harmonious passion,* and the second is called *obsessive passion*. The first one results in a high level of concentration/attention, and the second one results in the inability to create a difference between work and life. People with the second type of passion often feel burnout. They do not have any hobbies outside their work. Their work is their life.

Everything needs to be in harmony. Whenever there is dissonance, life tends to teach us a lesson. For entrepreneurs, it is in the face of burnout. While the entrepreneurs with harmonious passion feel taken by their work, they try to break from it and have flexibility. According to the Harvard review, they could balance their job with other activities in their lives without experiencing conflict, guilt, or adverse effects when not engaging in work.

Kevin Eschleman, an assistant professor of psychology at San Francisco State University, says that the more you engage in creative activities, the better you'll do at work. But how does one take out time for activities when you can't even remember to eat or drink water? I have an answer. If you continue to do that, you will soon experience burnout, and then you will be blank. You won't be able to work or rest. You'll be in limbo.

Now ask yourself, do you want to end up in such a situation where you can't work for your dear venture? If the answer is *no*, I suggest you start adopting self-care habits in your life.

"I make time and space to care for my mental health, I stopped setting my alarm for five a.m. and let myself sleep until I wake up naturally. I observe digital Sabbaths in which I stop checking email, keeping up with the news online, and checking into Foursquare. I travel less. I read and run more."
-Brad Feld, an American entrepreneur, dealing with his entrepreneurial depression

Just like Brad, you can try to bring small habits into your daily routine that can help you pause and unwind to relieve and prevent the toll of negative stress from compounding and then exploding and resulting in burnout. We all know that starting a business is not something you can do at the speed of light! It requires long hours and attention to the work, customers, and solving problems. You may find yourself busy on the weekends as well. As much as you want to spend time on your business, always remember that nothing is worth sacrificing your mental and physical health and loved ones.

With all the other things discussed in this chapter, always remember that the most important aspect of growing and scaling your business is to keep your health in check. It will take a lot of energy, attention, and ideas. Connect with your superpowers and not succumb to a depleted mind and fatigued body.

CHAPTER 8

RESOURCES FOR GROWTH

"One of the greatest skills of leadership is being unflappable. Anytime you do anything in the world, there's going to be criticism." **-Arianna Huffington, co-founder, and editor-in-chief of Huffington Post Media Group**

When it comes to the growth of a startup, the stories can be somewhat mythical. Look at Mark Zuckerberg. He failed in four applications before the launch of Facebook.[1] The first company that had a successful launch is Bill Gates's credit, who launched Microsoft when he was in his forties. The fact is, there is little to no evidence that the first startup a person creates reaps great benefits. Most people fail in launching startups. They learn from their mistakes and grow better, and do better the next time. The entrepreneur's journey is rampant with many problems, yet many have successfully started and developed their businesses.

Businesses launched in a recession are the foundation of modern society. In 1908, General Motors was established just before one of the greatest economic crises. It is now one of the most known and successful

---

[1] "104 Customer Service Statistics & Facts of 2021 [UPDATED]." Retrieved from (https://www.proprofs.com/c/customer-support/customer-service-statistics-facts-trends/)

companies in electrical supplies and products. Their success lies in their ability to remain relevant and sustain in the industry ebbs and flows in one of the most dynamic economies. The success of the business has little to do with making record-breaking numbers.

Real success focuses on an entrepreneur's ability to set goals, see the issues and find solutions to problems. But how will you find answers to the problems if you have never seen or experienced a problem that is bigger and outside of your box? The heel of success for the entrepreneur is experience – the second is the ability to think *BIG*. Before you dive into a business, understand your "why," what problem your business will solve, and market research to determine if consumers are buying what you are selling.

Does that mean you need to work in an office for two decades before you launch your business – No. More resources are available, and technology software allows entrepreneurs to start up quickly; whereas, some processes are still tedious. You will waste valuable years waiting for something to become a safe choice if you focus on the stars aligning perfectly in your niche or industry to take that leap. It is important to do your research and understand the industry from a critical perspective and learn how things are done quickly. Yes, you need industry experience, and you need to know the issues you will face in the long run.

Stagnation Is An Issue

Up to this point, I shared my ideas to stay afloat, the risk of getting stuck in a phase of your business versus expanding is a never-ending concern, and why some companies never excel to the next level. Coupled with external changes, recession, competition, and retaining loyal customers, these are constant concerns for entrepreneurs, business owners, and CEOs. A possible solution to these problems is to know your business, know your customers, and keep a keen eye on opportunities and solutions that will help you grow your business.

Here are a few major and common problems faced by entrepreneurs when they start a new business:

Value Proposition

The value proposition is a valid concern for today's business owner. Brian Chesky, the co-founder of Airbnb, once said, "If we tried to think of a good idea, we wouldn't have been able to think of a good idea. You just have to find the solution to a problem in your own life."

Your product or service you offer should feature ease of use. Most entrepreneurs think that they have to develop complex ideas, which is not always true. Simply, you have to create a product or service that is a better mousetrap. Let me give you an example. Grammarly and Hemingway App have millions of users because they were the first two products in a niche. Grammarly, back in 2010 when it launched, was truly under-planned. It used to be a correction plugin for Microsoft Word.

Hemingway App came after Grammarly as a website, where you could edit, arrange and review your content. Soon, Hemingway App gained much more traction with target consumers than Grammarly as Hemingway App offered more writing features. Understanding its declining competitive position in the market, Grammarly revamped its brand. It developed an add-on web-based App that helped the end-user with features similar to the Hemingway App model. Soon, Grammarly became a greater competitor of Hemingway App. By stepping back to improve their initial idea of a plugin for Microsoft Word, it produced a web-based App that is more commonly known than Hemingway.

The market competition you have to face is not always your enemy. Your competitor allows you to win the battle, not hinder your growth. You will have a better opportunity of growing your product or service if you do not throw in the towel every time competition comes to the market.

Entrepreneurs and business owners need to keep a sharp eye on their market if you don't want to be yesterday's news that the fisherman uses to wrap today's catch. The product or service that is popular today can quickly become irrelevant when your competitor makes a better mousetrap. It is imperative to maintain contact with your consumers through social media and direct outreach to understand what makes them buy your product or service over the competitor.

That is how today's business grows. When you launch a product or service, your competitor will use your model to launch a better one that is a 2.0 version of your product or service. Be prepared for your competition by making sure you keep a competitive edge.

Listen To Your Customers

Remember the Hemingway App versus Grammarly anecdote? The fact is, there are valuable lessons to learn from customer feedback. When Grammarly first launched its plugin, the feedback was that the product was not good. Grammarly ignored the feedback, and Hemingway App found the solution. Take time to listen to your customers before they dump you to find a better solution.

Today, having good customer service employees is crucial to your brand's growth. According to an article written by Riddhima Mathur, *104 Customer Service Statistics & Facts of 2021,* "When it comes to making a purchase, 64% of people find customer experience more important than price – Gartner. Customer support in today's marketplace is not a teenager sitting in the complaint center. Today's customer service experience is the future of your brand.

The lessons to learn from your customers are that brand and experience are your business's lifeline. Being mindful and aware of market changes is imperative to your survival.

Key takeaway: Listening to your customers is key to finding new customers and retaining current customers. Consumers value how they're treated, which is a key factor in their decision to buy your product or service.

As an example, take the Bright Iris Film Company. Lisa Trifone, founder and principal of Bright Iris Film Company believes great customer service requires more than a smile and upbeat energy. She dedicates time to understanding her customers' expectations and ways to exceed their expectations. Trifone says, "Investing the resources needed to learn more about your customers will deepen your connection, which makes them more inclined to choose your brand."

Value On Both Ends

If you want to have a successful venture, it must provide value on both ends. Your product or service must give your customers value and garner value from the product. Highlight useful features of your product for free and keep, equally or more, high-end features in the paid version of your product or service. The goal is to create value in your free version while promoting distinction and worthwhile investment in the paid features.

Prove What You Claim

It is essential that your product or service you are selling do what you advertise. Customers hate it when false advertisements deceive them. Sometimes, it's tough getting started, but this approach is not right. You will lose your current customers and not attract new customers who might buy your products and subscribe to your services. Shaddy businesses whose only goal is to scam buyers or use misleading content are running the risk of legal action.

Impact Matters

Your customers have the right to take action against businesses that make statements that are incorrect or likely to create a false impression about a product or service. Simply, it's not worth it. Treat your customers how you want to be treated as a customer.

Know Your Weaknesses

If a business owner does not understand its weaknesses, it has a risk that brings potential issues. There are times when you cannot see your business model's deficiencies. But you can use resources such as surveys and data reports to make sure that you are getting the right feedback. The data will outline key points of concern or dissatisfaction so you can begin working on them.

Reputation Matters

Companies are dealing with customers more directly than ever before. Again, customer service is the key to explaining your brand's quality to the consumers. Potential customers look at current customers' feedback, ratings, and how they are treated to see if they want to engage with a brand. Make sure that you are clear about your customer service standards. Social media, T.V. shows, publications, and other content creating entities rate products and services all the time. Be prepared to be polite and friendly, and take negative criticism as constructive feedback.

Other Perspectives Are Important

Instead of ruminating over low ratings and negative content, look for the silver lining to find lessons or insight that you can use to improve your service or product. Sometimes, it helps to step away – watch a movie, go for a hike, or go to an art gallery. A wise approach to problem-solving is putting the problem away for a little, allowing for fresh eyes and a clear head to be a part of your thought process.

When you come back to the problem with a fresh perspective, you will see solutions you may have missed before. Not to mention, being emotional about business and the related decisions is not a smart strategy. It is better if you see your option differently and if it is a way to salvage the situation.

Analyze Your Success Factor

As an entrepreneur, you are not always successful, but there are times when things work out. Keep an eye on the times and scenarios where sales are the easiest. That is a quick and straightforward way to know how to sell your product. It is going to look a bit dubious, but try to recreate the same scenario over and over again. One of my benchmarks is understanding why you lost a sale, learning your lessons; and, know why you won a deal, and repeat the winning formula.

To keep it real, measuring other obstacles often influence success factors. According to Benetrends Financials 2020 report, *Minority-*

Owned Businesses: Beyond Statistics, small businesses are still leading the way in startups, but some trends are still slow to change. Here are a few highlighted in this article:

- Despite the gains over the past decade, minority business owners are still less likely to receive small business loans than their non-minority business counterparts. The problem is worse for those with less than $500,000 in gross receipts.

- The average amounts of small business loans are smaller for the minority-owned company. For a minority business with over $500,000 in gross revenue, the average loan approval was $149,000. Non-minority business loans average $310,000. Interest rates are more often higher for a minority business.

- Many minority business owners assume rejection and fail to pursue small business funding when starting a small business.

In a down or booming economy, financial strength is a key factor in measuring your success.

Creditworthiness is a major asset in preparation for success. If you are in the stage of evaluating your product or service, now is the time to assess your creditworthiness. Your personal credit is used to determine your loan eligibility as a startup. Before you go full throttle in launching your business, meet with your banker to discuss funding options or a credit advisor to improve your credit score. To share my story, when I decided to launch my business, my personal credit was in the toilet because I missed payments, overused my credit cards to stay afloat when I was downsized from my corporate job. Before I hung my shingle, I decided to speak with a banker and fill out a loan application. I knew it would be rejected, but I used the experience to see what I needed to fix or have removed from my credit report.

The experience felt like getting a bad report from my doctor, who chastised me for a bad health report, but the time spent with my banker was well spent. Over three years, I worked with him to learn about something I needed as a lifeline for my company – business credit.

Like me, most startups start with passion, energy, and a desire to be their boss. Ideally, it is better to start your business with an investor to infuse money and offer the emotional distance needed to make professional decisions. However, this is not often the start of most women and minority-owned startups – we hustle, grit, and grind to make it happened. Along the way, though, you will need to cultivate trust and bond with influential people and investors. If you are lucky, you may meet someone who can take you to Wall Street.

Secondly, make sure you are practically equipped to deal with issues that may arise in the business development if you start your business with a friend.

These are a few basic and common points that women and minority-owned businesses do not commonly practice. We have seen too many brilliant and highly lucrative opportunities go to waste because the founder or business owner did not understand the venture's true potential. If I had to give one piece of advice to an entrepreneur or wise business owner, it would be, everything has value and can be *sold*. Timing and doing market research matter when deciding to start a business – start there.

If you have evaluated your product or service you have developed, you should be more inclined to work toward working or plan to achieve your goal with your blood, sweat, and tears. Product or service placement, attracting the right audience, and sending a welcoming message is the key to making sure that your goods sell and add to the bottom line.

Now that you know the main aspects of good entrepreneurship, it's time to discuss a few simple ways to improve the process of developing your venture.

Calibrate

Knowing when to calibrate is the key to a good business plan for execution. It means, rather than rolling the dice, you plan for the journey you will take. Most of the issues listed above for the startups come from understanding your journey. Most people are good at developing products or services, but they are terrible at understanding how to execute successfully.

Resource Management

Whether you are a startup or an established business, they both require resources. You cannot fulfill any contract or complete any project without cash flow and resources to support the effort. Here is where most entrepreneurs and small business owners struggle. I can share so many stories about a startup or a small business owner who wins a contract and they don't have the financial capacity to deliver the work to the contract terms. A common reaction is to panic and stress how they will meet the contract terms. Resource management is the best way for you to develop the capability and capacity to sustain you in the long run. As a startup, likely, you will not have an established office, but maybe the kitchen table or a corner in the basement. Initially, your startup or small business will run from a spreadsheet to track your expenses and labor cost. Despite your limitations, you have to find a way to ensure that you deliver your work while managing your overhead costs.

Here are a few most commonly used resources that are efficient for you to use.

Marketing

The more marketing efforts you make, the more likely you will attract customers and increase your revenue. Many social media and digital marketers can market your brand and your product to other businesses based on your marketing strategy. Attracting new customers and retaining existing customers are directly linked to your marketing strategies.

Digital marketing is the simplest and free way to promote your product or service. If you can create your content, you can virtually do all of the essential aspects of online digital marketing for free.

If you do not have a website, buy a domain, create a website, make a Facebook page, or create a good online identity, all are necessary to reach your customers and sell your product or service. You will get great value for your efforts when people show interest in your business.

Free trials are another effective way to get the right audience's attention. It may be an added benefit to attract and retain clients that stay long term.

Mentors

Whether you are a startup or an established small business, having a mentor in your life is a great asset. Their role is to tell you if you are not performing well. They will help you avoid mistakes and make better decisions about your business. For all the highs and lows you will experience, having a mentor helps you remain focused on your goal and not get detracted from the everyday hustle-bustle.

Free Tools

Free tools are also a great strategy to develop your brand and build your influence. There are also free tools for you and your team to try to make sure you are using tools to help you manage processes and systems to support operations and collect your data. These tools are basic, and keep in mind that you will need to use more advanced tools to integrate your processes and track all data metrics to measure the business's overall performance.

Google Drive Tools

Google Drive tools are an amazing set of free tools that are still free. From Google Drive to Google Docs, you can use these tools to share your documents, present your content professionally, and grow your audience.

If you have spreadsheet data, share it in Google Sheets. There are many ideas for how you can use them as an entrepreneur. You can use Google Calendar to set up meetings and make arrangements to have group calls.

Google Trends

Google Trends is a portal where the most trending topics appear on Google. If you are in a category like business or science, the portal will show you the most trending topics in that category. If you are developing marketing and commercial content, you will find Google Trends amazing. It will let you know all the hooks that will wrap up your audience and make them interested in your content.

If you are developing a calendar sheet, then the Google Trends portal will help you see all the ways you can use current affairs to your benefit. Google Trends is connected to Google News and will help you develop highly informed and well-balanced content for your clients.

HubSpot CRM

A CRM (Customer Relationship Management) is a system to help you track and manage sales and customer communication, contact activity, prospects, and sales conversions. HubSpot is a complete CRM platform with all the tools you need to grow better — whether you want to increase leads, accelerate sales, streamline customer service, or build a powerful website. As an example, one timesaver feature is how the technology links email communication in the CRM. Another feature is the alerts to let you know when your email was opened so you can gauge follow-up or the next step in your sales process. The benefits help you manage and deliver customer service and monitor customer engagement.

Outsourcing

Outsourcing is a great solution to help entrepreneurs and business owners to manage their labor costs. Here are the many ways how outsourcing helps entrepreneurs grow and manage their overhead costs effectively:

Cost Reduction

The cost of managing direct-hire is three fourth of any company's budget. This cost includes payroll, payroll taxes, worker's compensation, health insurance, Medicaid, unemployment insurance tax, state tax, and a few more. You can contain your labor costs by outsourcing and hiring employees using temp staffing agencies. For a pay rate plus the markup fee, temp agencies lower your labor costs (and risks) significantly. The downside of using a temp agency is finding top tier talent that is reliable and has the skills to help you grow and scale your business. A contingent workforce's upside is professionals who prefer contract or temp assignments in exchange for flexibility and work-life balance. You will need to make sure you know the legal parameters of joint employer status and employee ownership when using a temp agency. If you are considering, consider when choosing a temp agency:

Who hires or fires the employee?

Who supervises and controls the employee's work schedule or employment conditions to a substantial degree?

Who determines the employee's rate and method of payment?

Who maintains the employee's employment records?

The answers to these questions will help you evaluate the pros and cons of hiring talent internally or partnering with a temp agency to outsource this need.

Diverse Talent Pool

As previously stated, labor costs are one of the most expensive allocations for any company – whether you are a startup or an enterprise. To manage this overhead expenditure, USA employers are using global markets to hire or contract talent worldwide, sometimes at a fraction of the cost, work as a remote employee or contractor, or relocate them to the USA using a work visa. A few other resources entrepreneurs and startups use to complete short-term gigs or projects are FIVVER, Freelancer, and UpWork. You can get outstanding services at a much lower price if you are willing to outsource your needs.

Get Down to Business

When you are running your business, most of your time should be devoted to business strategies to build, grow, scale the company, and manage your leadership team to ensure operations are getting the job done. Whether your talent was hired in-house, using a temp agency, or hiring contractors directly, you will still need to ensure the work is getting done. It is important to have technology tools to monitor performance and results. By doing so, you will have more time to be about the business to expand your footprint and brand to attract new customers and retain existing customers.

Resource Planning

It is critical to know the value of resource planning in managing, growing, and scaling a business. Whether you have a business plan or not, taking time for resource planning allows you to forecast expenditures, project timelines, and key result areas (KRAs) to measure impact and outcomes. From the legal aspects to the financial burden, being an entrepreneur or business owner is an extensive and complex mission. KRAs are useful, and good reasons to fortify your business operations and systems are imperative to measure and track performance and success.

Joint Venture

A joint venture is like a marriage – do your vetting first before you sign on the dotted line. When a joint venture is a win-win for both parties, this venture can help grow a business without working yourself to death. Gone are the days when a business owner was expected to work alone and build a conglomerate from scratch. Today's businesses come together to collaborate as one global community. Here are the four beneficial ways that a joint venture can help you expand your company.

Franchise

Franchises are the best if you provide unique value. For example, Ali Baba has a business model that was new and coveted in Asia. It grew in China, became a formidable force, and then started franchising in Pacific Asia and South Asia. The main focus was to ensure that the business grew in regions where their services were needed and appreciated. You will find much better examples of franchises in your surroundings as well.

For example, twenty years ago, KFC and McDonald's grew and expanded in the whole world. Yes, McDonald's and KFC are famous in the U.S., but they genuinely have a stronghold in Asia and Africa because these were new and unthought-of products when they were introduced in these regions.

Franchising is the most common way for small businesses to grow, especially software brands. Samsung franchised its business worldwide to get its phones on every shelf in the world. The same business model is followed by Apple, Nokia, and many more brands.

Careem, a subsidiary of Uber, was launched the year it spread out to entire Asia. Depending on your appetite for growth, franchising is an option to grow quickly and globally. Franchising offers many opportunities to expand to attract more customers, increase revenue, and boost profit margins. If you are considering a joint venture, it is worthwhile the time and consultation to engage a lawyer to help you make the right decisions for your business. Subsidiary

When a company is linked to your company's name but is an independent company known as a subsidiary, the positive impact of considering a subsidiary is that you can start a completely new venture and take advantage of tax laws and tax breaks.

Let's suppose you know a competitor whose business has grown through adding subsidiaries to the parent company. They do not call it a company. They call it a subsidiary. If you do your research, you may find that setting up as a subsidiary offers advantages that include its entity, employees, and other aspects of operating as a subsidiary. The parent company is still the owner of the subsidiary that operates separately. If you decide to grow your business using subsidiaries, contact a CPA to understand possible tax liabilities, financial burdens, and potential legal liabilities.

Individuals found the concept of independent ownership and leveraging subsidiary as a great way to expand their businesses under the umbrella of bigger firms. Subsidiaries are a great idea if you believe in the potential of this type of business model and control. Suppose you are an entrepreneur who wants complete autonomy, but you like the franchise model. In that case, you should consider becoming an owner of your company and turn your venture into your subsidiary.

Acquisition

An acquisition is simply the purchase of another company. In a down or up economy, acquisitions can be positive or negative growth – it depends on many factors discovered during the evaluation phase. A common thought is that selling a company implies negative connotations. In today's market, acquisitions are considered a competitive advantage and approach to building capability and capacity. The most recent example consumers know the acquisition of Instagram was recently bought out by Facebook, and so was WhatsApp.

As a business owner or entrepreneur, weigh the advantages and disadvantages of building a company to own or sell. If you are interested in acquiring companies to expand or sell your company, you will be wise to determine the benefits.

Acquisitions may be *BIG* move to grow if you are a company with promising statistics and single or majority ownership. If you do your due diligence the blend the assets of the acquired company to create a better brand name, then your company has a chance to become a better competitor. When Uber in South Asia bought out Careem, it strengthened Careem's standing as not only a copycat of Uber but also as a formidable competitor.[2]

Merger

When a company struggles to stay afloat or needs help to remain relevant, an option to consider is a merger. What is the difference between mergers and acquisitions? The acquisition means the new company owns all the rights. It can keep or reject any regulations or staff that the original company has and vice versa.

Mergers are a good idea when a company's product or service can strategically expand the brand or footprint. If you like a product or service and it is already established, then you will buy the company. Mergers are usually done between larger, financially established

---

[2] "Uber Completes Acquisition of Careem." Retrieved from (https://investor.uber.com/news-events/news/press-release-details/2020/Uber-Completes-Acquisition-of-Careem/default.aspx).

companies that will join a struggling company. In a down economy, small companies shop for merger opportunities to keep you from going out of business.

Entrepreneurship and business ownership are two sides of the same coin. You either grow as an entrepreneur to the point that a major company buys your business, or you grow to the point that your business starts acquiring other businesses. The only difference is whether you are growing or merely surviving.

Surviving for a long time is not worth much. If you sell your business when it still has positive cash flow and can show a net profit, this is attractive to potential buyers and a good reason to sell based on the evaluation. Before you consider a merger, take time to do your research and vet interested parties who want to buy your product or service. I can't say this often enough, but seek the advice of a corporate attorney with experience in facilitating mergers and acquisitions., This chapter's main focus is to show that certain aspects of business ownership can make you or break you.

Along with understanding your business's financial side, an entrepreneur or business owner needs to be astute and have certain personal strengths and CEO competencies that we have discussed throughout this chapter. The second half of the chapter has focused on making a business successful. A good company focuses not only on opening the shop and sitting in it. It also focuses on ensuring that the company has a sufficient survival rate. You cannot achieve that if you spend all your time *in the business and not about the business*. If this is your approach, you will lose sight of the company with your head down dealing with the day-to-day tactical things.

Your first course of action is to build your team, so they will allow you to focus on executing the business strategy and building out the sales strategy- customers and revenue.

CHAPTER 9

TALENT FOR GROWTH

Any company that has gone from keeping three employees to having 3,000 workers knows how to make the employees a part of company growth. If you do not know how to grow your employees, you cannot help but watch your company suffer. You have to learn how to make the best use of your employees to make a good company.

In my opinion, there are two types of business owners. If you know how to turn employee growth into company growth, you are one step ahead to expand your enterprise. Let me make it very clear, the second type of employers do not last a long time. They end up having conflicting strategies between leveraging their human capital and financial capital – either way, the business lags considerably in getting things done. I will discuss how to grow your employees and the business simultaneously in two ways: social and corporate engagement.[3]

Social Engagement for Productivity

Here are a few basic principles about social interaction to keep in mind when trying to get your employee to engage with your workplace.

---

[3] "The Impact of Employee Engagement on Business Growth." *Happier*. Retrieved from (https://www.happierco.com/blog/employee-engagement-company-growth/).

Employee Satisfaction

Employee satisfaction relates to small matters that employees come across every day. Always notice if more than two employees make the same complaint, whether it is about people, work culture, or the workplace.

When your employees have a problem with the company's benefits or policies, it's time to look into the problem. The wise thing to do is look at whether bad actors are being counterproductive to disrupt the culture. To diffuse potential large-scale problems, survey your workplace often and routinely listen to the complaints. Major complaints that are ignored can create a perception by other employees that there is a company morale problem. The more you let a problem lie, the likely it causes discourse. Remember, there is power in the numbers.

If people try to gang up, focus on making sure that they do not think it will end in their favor. But if two separate employees who are not necessarily linked socially and voice the same problem, it is time to look into that problem. Whether they are about the commute or the workplace culture, everyday issues can significantly impact how an employee sees their workplace. Make sure these small issues do not collect to become larger ones.

Productivity Threshold

What is productivity? Is it the quality of the work an employee does or the quantity of the work an employee delivers? It's a subtle combination of both aspects. But you have to make your employees understand that they are expected to provide both quality and quantity of the assigned work. The benefit is to help them understand how the delivery and quality of work come together.

A simple tip for this is to start an employee with small assignments and observe their ability to take on more complex projects. If an employee wants only to perform small tasks, they will likely not have the drive to grow and maybe a "steady Eddie." Either way, allow employees time to let them understand and accept responsibility for the quality of work they are expected to deliver.

Low Turnover

Ensure that you build a company and ecosystem with a low employee turnover. When a workplace does not retain its talent over time, it also struggles with momentum. If you have to choose between reassigning an employee or letting them go, exhaust your options to consider reassignment. This option of flexibility will help other employees feel more relaxed and engaged. They will think that their value and contribution are counted.

Creativity

Try to avoid discouraging new ideas. It is a more worthwhile use of time when there are parameters and how creativity is a resource for achieving its goals. If the company encourages creativity, it is not uncommon for employees to develop ideas – some new and others not so new – to management. Many small businesses incentivize employees to generate ideas that benefit the company – it's call intrapreneurship. Companies use this to create a new business or venture within the company, and it may become a subsidiary. Intrapreneurship is very common among I.T. and magazine companies.

Creativity can be beneficial by assigning a mentor to help employees by listening ear to the employees and facilitating their ideas by providing direction and support.

Revenue Generation

Revenue generation is the most challenging task that the business owner can have. The most talented employees are not worth the pay if they cannot deliver the needed results. It is worthwhile to make sure employees are trained in providing client satisfaction.

Client satisfaction and retention can only be achieved if the upper management has honed in on the process. If upper management is clueless about keeping the clients, they will be silent even if they know the secret recipe. To remedy this, make sure you are clearly defining the culture for retaining clients and acquiring new clients. Businesses that find client acquisition challenging will probably struggle badly in other parts of the operations.

Expansion Issues

If you start a company with several workers and have no prior experience managing employees, expanding may be challenging. As your company grows, your workplace will require a more robust structure. Here is a list of major challenges[4] that business owners and entrepreneurs face when deciding to expand the company:

The 25th Employee Problem

The communication system starts falling apart once you reach the 25th employee in your company growth plan. Once you have 25 employees, you will see that employee communication will become more complex. The times you used to have lunch with your employees now becomes a challenge to remember every employee's name. You have to come up with ways for employees to connect with management.

---

[4] "Why Everything Breaks When You Reach 25 Employees." *Get Lighthouse*. Retrieved from (https://getlighthouse.com/blog/company-growth-25-employees/).

Firstly, whether you are a brick-and-mortar company, virtual, or a combination of both, create portals where all general announcements and regular updates are posted. All employees should have a system of accepting communication for them. This software is plentiful or easy to create within the company. It is wise to have online project management software like Trello and others. These kinds of Apps allow project managers to closely track project development and provide a setup where all the work and related employees are in sync. This App will also allow the project manager to control their job and finish projects to an expected timeline.

Understand Delegation

Delegation is a science. It does not mean that your subordinates are going to vanish into thin air for three weeks and appear with the perfect project. You have to develop a delivery system to communicate and mark expected milestones. Do not let your teams vanish for a week. Ask them to share the progress every day.

Having milestones is a benefit to help you monitor the project's completion and a guard rail when the employees are not performing well or simply if one member or several of them are not working out. A greater benefit is that you will see the employee work in real-time. Try and make sure new employees' work comes to you in the first 90 days to see how they have progressed over time - do they have the right skills or require the skills needed.

Left on the Sideline

Lack of updates, missing memos, and not being invited into meetings are both excuses and valid reasons for feeling left out. Have a company protocol for these issues. H.R. should monitor feedback sessions and have clear policies for inclusion and communicative interactions to ensure that all department heads are accountable for employee interactions and relationships.

The supervisors should be incentivized to work with their employees. There should be a strong push for the supervisors' team to help new employees become acclimated, develop relationships, and access resources to help new employees engage. This approach is a great way to make sure employees and supervisors work in sync to deliver their results.

Career Growth

How many times have you seen a situation where an employee appears to struggle in getting a promotion or pay raise? They have to work hard to get it, and when the time comes, their pay raise is postponed. Practices such as this causes disgruntle behavior among employees. Always try to find a way to work fairly with your employees. If you have an employee who has outgrown their job, make sure that the employee feels free to bid on a new position.

If the employee is trying but cannot get above average results, see if a transfer to another department may help – N.B.A. teams do it all the time. These matters require an H.R. professional to manage more than recruiting and onboarding. If you have an H.R. team that can grow and develop the workforce, the company will grow and become stronger. Talented employees who leave the company and thrives with another company and with a competitor should be a concern for you. Be mindful and focus on creating a workplace that embraces change and agility.

Toxic Culture

A culture that negates the employees' growth is the worst option for you to allow in your company. You must understand that the entire workplace, sustenance, and other aspects must align to ensure employees have a good experience. If the employees do not have a good experience, then it is a fault that should be corrected.

Most employers are cautious about making their employees a priority because it may seem counterproductive. But your company is as good as the employees you have. We have all heard the story about the C.E.O. walking into a local Amazon store and seeing the employee sleeping on the couch. He simply took a photo of the employee and posted it with a quote. The picture ended up being good publicity and demonstrated that employees felt comfortable in their skin and the employer and employee relationship was a win-win.

It is always a good thing to share your experience, ideas, and goals with the employees to give them a positive vibe. The simple fact is that when you have many employees with various backgrounds and mindsets, all of them are not going to fit into one kind of box that will be the same experience for everyone. If you develop a culture of working with and appreciating your diverse resources, I believe you will see company growth that will amaze others.

Have Quarterly Check-in Sessions

Make sure you, your managers, or H.R. leader sit with every employee two or three times a year. If an employee is disengaged and shows interest in leaving, have a sit-down and ask how they feel. Ask them for honest feedback. If employees leave due to incivility, discrimination, or bullying, the manager and the team should be retrained. The point is incivility, bullying, and discrimination are very serious issues that lead to severe talent losses. These issues make you liable for allegations or legal claims of harassment, and the fines will make you think about the times you ignored these problems. It is imperative that you make sure that your leadership team builds a workplace free of discrimination, harassment, and other behaviors that create a toxic workplace. Workplace toxicity is an epidemic. Once your employees perceive or believe it is expected of them to behave that way, many of them are apt to adopt these behaviors and perpetuate these behaviors as they advance in the company ecosystem.

Show Up and Repeat Many Times

You want your employees to come to work and be on time. One way to encourage this preferred behavior is to post the importance of attendance, communicate the policy and consequence. Making this policy visible communicates your business value for attendance and the expectations you have for employees to be present and available to serve the customers.

Your employees will understand the work culture by setting up your workplace. Ensure your corporate policies, culture, evaluation process, and other aspects of employee performance and relations show the workers that all the company's policies and practices are strongly upheld.

Celebrate Successes

Successes are great even when they come in small packages. You have to understand that the success of a new employee getting acclimated is so important to them and the company. Applauding their success and allowing them to grow will give you a return on your investment to recruit and hire more employees – it really pays off in the long run. Candidates seeking a job that incentivizes and challenges their thinking will attract them to join your team, and they will likely experience satisfaction in their careers and be happy employees. If your junior employees think that their work is just a blip in the vast amount of data collected, they will act like that. Your greatest responsibility is to make sure that employees feel that their contributions are part of a bigger picture and help them feel proud of their company's journey.

Learn to Transition

Transitions in the journey of a company are an inevitable fact. You will open a new department. You will have to downsize, relocate, pivot, or launch new branches. All of these are transitions that may be unsettling for your employees. Learn to deal with their fears and make sure you have strong leaders in place.

One way to manage transitions is to break the changes into phases and find a way to fix any problems before you move to a new phase. When the issues move from one phase to another, they become bigger than before and grow into serious problems. Make sure you are using and monitoring fallout and troubleshooting regularly.

Incentive Plans

Incentives entice the employees to perceive your business as a fair workplace. Incentives that connect with the employees are the best way to get high employee engagement. Incentives are the key to award performance that impacts productivity, its growth, and the employees feel the incentives are attainable. Let's put it in a real-life example. If you eat twice a day, you will not feel very eager for the monthly feast. As employees are incentivized regularly, they will not feel the need to work so hard and burnout trying to achieve a pay raise awarded at the end of the year. Here are a few incentive ideas to try in your workplace:

Right Hiring

The first incentive for your H.R. team and managers is to collaborate and ensure the right hiring. Make sure the skills needed in a job are vetted in the candidate you hire. If you hire a new employee for a job and s/he cannot perform the essential duties, the team will perceive him/her like dead weight. Soon, it is likely you will observe the employee will fail to engage and loses interest in performing the work, and things will spiral downward from here.

Training for Growth

Have a training system in place for your employers can access as needed to learn new skills to meet work demands. If you have good onboarding and mentorship programs, your employees will adapt quickly. Training is the best way to onboard, develop, and build a talent pool that can succeed and scale with its growth and demands.

30-60-90 Day Program

This type of program is designed to help employees understand the ecosystems that make up the organization. Have a process in place for employees to get through orientation policies, practices, systems, and other communication important to acclimating and fitting into their new job. This approach will help them better understand their value add to the company.

Open Communication

When employees receive a sudden surprise about their performance, they can receive the worst experience. There is a difference between positive reinforcement and managing the performance review like a hidden agenda. If your employee ever asks you directly about their performance, schedule time to share the good, the bad, and the truth. That simple fact is that it will allow them to trust and communicate with you.

Encouraging Teamwork

Teamwork makes the dream work – so cliché, but it is true. No one person gets the glory, but there is so much more to teams than just saying the phrase. In fact, think about all the time, effort, and cost to build effective teams. Many studies show companies who invest in team building enjoy higher productivity, higher profits, and better customer satisfaction. Small businesses should also invest in teambuilding to benefit the company's future growth and success. Your employees need to know when they work together, it pays. When a team player takes a new employee under their wing and show them how to fit in, it's a win-win.

This one example is an idea that can motivate your entire company to help new employees to join up and engage with the company. If you want them to strive toward growth, you have to strive for that, too. Make sure your workplace encourages people, with a variety of incentives, to work together and promote each other so that your company grows and builds a sustainable future.

Happy Hour

Happy hour is time allowed for other than ten-minute breaks that your employees are free to take during a workday. Happy hour is a great benefit that is accrued and awarded to all employees. The hours can be used to engage in volunteer or other leisure or community activities that are fun and relaxing for them and their family. It is not a big financial burden and a great way to impact your work culture. It makes employees feel cared for and shows your support for other things that benefit the community, nature, or social programs. They will also think that they have personal freedom, which is a great morale booster for all employees.

Out-of-the-box Benefits

There are many culturally appropriate out-of-the-box incentives you can give. You can give off for observed holidays or the option of working from home. You can provide perks such as movie tickets, store discounts, and vouchers that employees can use or share with others. All of these incentives will help you gain stronger traction with the employees. When employees feel appreciated, they will be more open to making more efforts to perform beyond the minimum requirements.

Rewards and Recognition

Rewards and recognition are valuable when they don't lose their value. Have guidelines for managers to follow when giving rewards or recognition. For one policy, employees have to exceed a set of standards or KPIs to be recognized and rewarded. When it appears that the company uses favoritism or the "halo effect" to determine recognition and rewards, employees will lose interest and distrust management and H.R.

Before an employee receives a reward or recognition, make sure you know and follow your H.R. guidelines and selection criteria.

Work-Life Balance

Every employee needs a work-life balance. A great return on your investment of time and resources is to have a goal to implement a health and wellness plan that rewards health, not endless overtime. A way to make sure that work-life balance is encouraged in the workplace is to limit how overtime is used. If an employee is working overtime, it can only be for important reasons. Working a few hours of overtime might be necessary to meet demand once in a while. Still, employee health needs to balance work and personal time pay off to minimize health risks. Problems such as stress, workplace accidents, repetitive motion injuries, and associated lifestyle conditions are also a health risk for the company.

Exit Interviews

Many business owners and entrepreneurs don't understand the value of exit interviews. It is common for a new client to ask me, "Why are we interviewing a person who is leaving the company?"

An exit interview is a valuable survey that gathers feedback about the company or coworkers' issues to determine if there is a problem or if the job was a bad fit.

In some cases, many companies like the option to rehire their old employees if they leave on good terms. Talented employees may consider re-employment depending on how they were treated when they left their employment. If you develop a culture of making sure that employees feel heard when leaving, calling them back could be easy and a benefit. In any case, make sure you know how the employee felt and what their issues were that caused them to resign. Valid issues that cause talented employees to leave should be a concern to retain future employees hired to add value to the company.

Employee Compensation

Employee pay may include base salary, wages, incentives, and/or commission, depending on several factors. In deciding the best strategy, understand your compensation strategy and how it meets the business needs and the company brand. If you are a startup or a small business, it is not cost-effective to compete with large companies. However, remember the benefits you offer job seekers to work in a small company. Here is a chart to compare:

Large Companies	Small Companies
• Lots of Perks	• Nimble
• More Technology	• Lots of Opportunities
• Predictable Workplace	• Sense of Community
• Structure & Order	• Access to the business owner/C.E.O.
• Job Security	• Flexible Workplace

As a startup or small business, you may not compete with large companies on salary but think about creative ways to attract and retain key employees. Do not underestimate the value of the advantages that your company has to offer that may not be readily available in larger companies.

CHAPTER 10
INVESTMENT IN GROWTH

When companies consider growth, they think of expansion, franchising, increasing their workforce, acquiring a new company, or investing in marketing strategies. But these may not be the best ways for a small company to grow. The best way to prepare your company for growth is to invest in it internally. I discussed Careem in chapter eight, so let's elaborate using Careem in this second discussion point.

Careem, a subsidiary of Uber, used Uber's work model. Careem started in the U.A.E., mainly in Egypt and Dubai. It was operating in the same market like Uber and had no way to distinguish itself from competitors. The only distinction it could create was to develop a business model that boasts the Uber business model to Eastern countries.[5]

Careem Focused on the most common issue in the Eastern world. Women could not get into rides without information about the driver. Careem solved this problem by verifying all the drivers' background checks and allowing the riders to have information about the drivers.

---

[5] "Dubai-Based Ride-Hailing Startup Careem Took on Uber—and Won." Retrieved from (https://www.fastcompany.com/90248563/how-a-middle-east-startup-took-on-uber-and-won).

This simple change led to a huge influx of women riders who were more comfortable using Careem. Other adaptations focused on customer service, which showed Careem much more accountability than Uber in the Asian regions. But these simple steps led to the company becoming a formidable competitor in the industry and with tech giants.

The simple fact is that your company will likely best if you focus on how to optimize your operations. A successful business is designed to ensure that customers are inclined to buy from them when it ran well. If you find the balance between four critical factors that define your business and all of your assets come together in sync, you will have profitable business operations.

Your greatest asset to leverage growth is *YOU*. In this chapter, I will share several ways for you to define a leadership plan to leverage your strengths, accentuate your brand, and how to develop a deeper understanding of your innate talents to create a growth plan to harness your company's future.

Leadership Traits

Leadership has been extensively discussed in the previous chapters. But those chapters focused on the impact you will have as a leader on your employees and how your organization structure impacts your growth factor. Here, I will discuss a leadership plan that focuses on *your* growth and development as a C.E.O. The following traits can have a powerful impact on your growth capacity, so make sure you learn and master these traits.[6]

---

[6] Llopis, Glenn. n.d. "The 12 Crucial Leadership Traits Of A Growth Mindset." *Forbes*. Retrieved from (https://www.forbes.com/sites/glennllopis/2018/04/24/the-12-crucial-leadership-traits-of-a-growth-mindset/).

Keep an Open Mind

The toughest challenge in growing your company is keeping an open mind.[7] In the year 2019, the world spent $3,360 billion on technology. Most businesses struggle with major workplace changes as technology takes over. Managers are overwhelmed with technology like Trello and the online information world. These are highly complex, algorithmic concepts dominating the workplace to manage widespread information.

The conundrum is understandable. Technology has turned the concept of basic marketing strategies upside down, and now we are learning digital marketing. The R.O.I. is now tracked, measure using a computer, and performance is becoming more tangible; numbers are easier to produce to measure traction and return on investment. Regarding global competition, the world is growing smaller by the second. But it is prudent to have an open mindset, so focus on being agile and willing to embrace many changes that we can all expect.

It is good to create research and development relationships with software and technology companies to try new technologies before investing to purchase. Some companies will give away new software or technology if you are willing to beta test features and give feedback regarding ease of use and functionality. Always try new software, service, or online technologies with a small team of seniors and end-user workers before you buy, and conduct focus groups to gather their feedback.

I have seen small companies make critical mistakes when they do not take the time to troubleshoot new technologies before they are

---

[7] "150+ Technology Statistics You Must Know: 2020/2021 Market Share Analysis & Data." *Financesonline.Com.* Retrieved from (https://financesonline.com/technology-statistics/).

deployed across the whole company. *Each time you fail to beta-test new technologies before deployment, the risk of eroding or comprising data integrity is highly probable.* Have a control team to test and document the features you are buying to solve a problem.

Do Not Fear Change

Technology is going to change the world for the better or worse. Modern transportation will allow people to travel hundreds of miles in less than an hour and share information at lightning speed. The billions of tech devices around the world connected to the Internet, all collecting and sharing data, called the Internet of Things (IoT) and Artificial Intelligence (A.I.), are two aspects that will impact how businesses mind data, do analytics and compete for market share. It is better to have a relevant and competitive mindset instead of becoming a relic.

Take COVID-19, for example. Who knew that we would end up working from home for the next couple of years? The virus was not even on the radar of many companies until January, and still, then, most were trying to operate "business as usual." In the fallout, some of us learned how to be resilient and identify ways to pivot our business to seize opportunities to meet new demands. Some closed their business under these circumstances, while others learned how to reinvent their business model to adapt to stay afloat. No one can blame employers who had to let good employees go because they could not generate the same revenue.

What if you are a small business that sells custom designed stationery, and your orders have drastically declined, and you are finding it difficult to sell your current products? As an example of resilience and pivoting, perhaps you can custom design disposable face masks with logos, team mascots, or inspirational quotes to uplift the human spirit.

Perhaps you can engage a group of your customers to be a part of your pivot effort to keep them engaged with your business. If you can find a little white space in your mind to be innovative, you can recreate your business to fill a need. Although it may be a long-shot idea, most companies that stayed afloat tend to go for unconventional long-shot ideas. Perhaps this example will tap into your innovation and creativity to take a risk to stay afloat when the economy takes a downward spiral.

Read the Tea Leaves

Was the 2008 meltdown predictable? Yes, many companies who predicted the downfall also faded away in the aftermath. Why? Because knowing when a catastrophe will arrive is not the same as being ready to face the music. Are you worried? Do you have a contingency or a disaster recovery plan? If you are not an experienced reader of tea leaves, sound business practices to recover is imperative to your survival in a down economy or to recover from a disaster.

Be Ready

Whether it is a natural disaster, pandemic, or a down economy, getting your business ready to open or ramp up again can be overwhelming.

Whether you decide on a full-scale reopening or a modified schedule, this process requires careful planning to minimize risks. Especially small businesses are eager to resume operations to generate revenue. Be careful thought is required to consider various risk factors for the company, employees, and consumers.

For a business to successfully reopen, here are a few things to consider:

1) Do you have a safety plan to minimize risks?

2) Have you thought through the details to resume the business operations, and

3) Do you have a plan to relaunch your business to encourage consumer confidence?

These three questions can only be addressed by developing a thorough, comprehensive business resumption plan and managing the potential business disruptors. Being ready is not about the breakout moment. It is about rebuilding the capital, infrastructure, goals, and business strategies that you will need to relaunch your business.

If you choose to shift your business and work from home, you will still need a strategy to execute a scaled-down company.

The message here is to proceed with caution to resume your business. Start with and focus on the products that sell or do exceptionally well to generate revenue. As the company stabilizes, add more products and services from your portfolio. If you try to do it all and resume full operations, this approach could be dangerous for your employees and customers.

Just as vital as all of the measures and protocols we mentioned for the physical reopening, keep in mind the need to put real effort behind your employees' and customers' emotional needs and wellbeing. Find creative ways to keep a personal connection with your customers and employees to encourage communication and feedback.

When you create a plan to open your doors, frequently communicate with their customers, and take steps to gain their confidence, and when you do, your recovery will be sustainable.

Lead With Confidence

As a leader, can you change your mind? Yes, but you have to consider the impact. If you told your employees to cancel a shipment, and your directive was a mistake, you cannot act like the cancellation is your employee's mistake. Mixed messages kill trust.

When you as a leader say one thing, and then you do another, it kills confidence and credibility. Mixed messages also demotivate your people and undermine your company's mission and vision.

A few examples of mixed messages are (1) when you promote excellence but tolerate poor performance, (2) when you set goals for the company but don't provide the resources to achieve them, and (3) when you say empower your team to make decisions, but you scold them when they make a decision that is a mistake. When your words and actions are misaligned, you're sending a mixed message. Your creditability is damaged, and your trust is compromised.

Lead by Example to Earn Respect

If your team loses a client, you lose a client. When employees think they will be hanged for a bad idea or mistake, they are less inclined to develop a good idea for fear of reprisal.

Whether you are a small business or a large enterprise, employees expect more trust, transparency, ethics, collaboration, and concerns for their needs. Just because you- are the C.E.O. or business owner doesn't mean that you have earned respect – we take our title and authority for granted. Leaders are challenged even more to lead by example for what they want from their employees. Start with a shift in mindset and become aware of mixed messages and the effect and influence they have on the employees and the organization as a whole.

Leading by example to earn trust starts with being more engaged by listening and becoming more involved by choosing opportunities to engage and connect with the team rather than expecting others to be examples. Be more mindful of your actions and words and how your team perceives you.

Grow with Your Team

It's not uncommon that most C.E.O.s and business owners are consumed with the complexities of running the day-to-day operations and responding to critical issues. Leading any sized organization in today's economy is a challenging endeavor. It is not unusual for the C.E.O. to invest in their leaders' development, but they seldom think about investing in their development. No matter how brilliant your idea or solution for a problem, if you are not investing in your development, you will always lose to the C.E.O. who is more competitive and recognizes the value of their skills to grow their business.

Be mindful of your blind spots that can hold you back from being your best self and how they impact the organization, your leaders, and employees. To create a company where employees proactively address their blind spots, commit to acknowledge your blind spots and how they impact your growth.

Invest in Potential

Have you ever been approached by a person down on their luck but looking for someone willing to give them a chance? What happens to me many times. Some talented people do not come from the best schools or have the finances to go to college. Some gifted people are not fit to go to college and learn in that environment. With all the assessments candidates have to endure to get a job, the process can mean defeat for talented but not the norm.

Many people who had to accept a job to flip burgers in a fast-food restaurant are often cast and limited to do this type of work. However, if you can see their potential, it may be a gamble but a worthwhile investment to give them a chance to unpack the talent hidden away for a great opportunity.

These are a few of the many reasons to consider talent cut from a different mold. In my experience, an act of social justice has been a win-win for me, my business, and the employee.

Avoid Silos

Growing up in the south, seeing a silo on a farm was a wonder to see. It was a red tall, round dome structure with no windows and tubes to release the stored grain. Silos are essential to farmers to protect their grain but an obstacle when it crops up in a business. When teams resist sharing information and resources, they create barriers such as turf tending, power struggles, fear, and performance inefficiencies. Silos also destroy trust, limits communication, and fosters a status quo mentality.

When an organization operates in a siloed structure, the company loses its ability to be agile and competitive to seize opportunities and pivot when necessary. When a business cannot make data-driven decisions, it impacts teamwork, customer service, sales, and the bottom line. When information isn't freely shared, your business can't make informed, data-driven decisions. Inventory, supply chain, distribution, marketing, and sales suffer when teams don't collaborate. One study revealed that professionals and executives' silo thinking shapes 70% of the customer experience. Breaking down that resistance saves money and makes it possible to meet company goals.[8]

---

[8] https://www.simplus.com/solutions-solve-silo-mentality/

Managers tend to favor silos of thought because they allow employers to get organized feedback from their employees. But silos are the killers of creativity and a source of bias workplace practices.

It is good to know how teams work and how internal engagements and interactions are managed.

A critical reason to break up silos is the customer experience. The following illustration shows the customer experience:

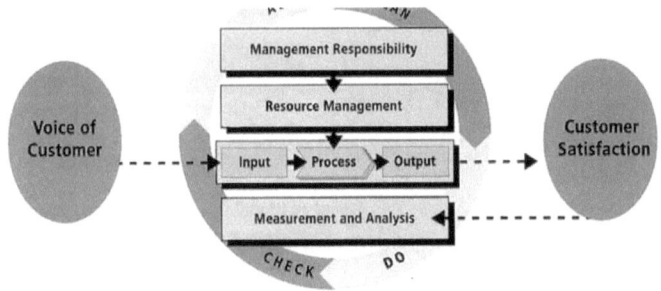

Image Credit: Business2Community

Having the customer experience the reason to dismantle silos and breaking down walls can be replaced with collaboration, trust, efficiencies, and better management of resources.

Be Inclusive

Not only are there issues involving the color of the skin, age, gender, or sexual orientation, but there are also age, race, and gender biases. Diversity, inclusion, and equity are becoming a very relevant issue globally and a worthwhile effort to address how division and polarization impact the bottom line. More companies are investing, and there are many business cases and research to validate the value and return for implementing this business strategy.

It is expected that most small and medium-sized businesses do not have a diversity, inclusion, and equity (DE&I) strategy to address biases within their organization. Secondly, most small businesses don't have an H.R. department to focus on policies, practices, and talent hiring hiring hiring. Instead of engaging a trained professional, the business owner or C.E.O. typically conveys why DE&I is important and champions engagement. The success of employees and leaders adopting the goals often yield a low return. The challenge is managing the implementation. If not handled well, the experience may cause greater discourse.

For the C.E.O. or business owner who is not a trained professional, understand the value for this business strategy: (1) tapping into diverse talent pools improve innovation and creativity, (2) your company expands its reach to serve the customers in the communities you serve, and (3) the moral position to remove barriers that limits diversity, inclusion, and equity is the right thing to do.

Embrace Change and Flexibility

Most companies are afraid of adapting to changing times and prefer to hold on to old cultural norms. Women have broken the veil of resistance to work and climb the corporate ladder.

Sheryl Sandberg once wrote in her book *Lean In*[9] about an incident where one of her good-natured, elderly bosses kept saying that she was perfect for his sons. Her comments on the issue were kind, and she explained that women should learn to be ice and dismissive in these instances. Her book explains how men try to appropriate the women into their lives when they make such comments. But at the end of the day, such sentiments are unfair.

---

[9] Anon. 2021. *"Lean In." Wikipedia.* http://en.wikipedia.org/wiki/Lean_In

Another common occurrence is to ask if the woman will continue to work at every milestone of her personal life. When she gets engaged, she is asked if she will continue to work. When she gets married or has a child, she is asked the same question. Perhaps, rather than waiting for a useful and high-quality employee to leave the workplace the moment it is culturally appropriate to suggest so, companies should ask themselves if they will be at a loss when they lose the employee? They should be more concerned about if they offer benefits and policies that protect the woman's job and allows for work-life balance, and have best practices such as onsite daycare, work-from-home, work share, and other similar options, which are all a few great ways to make sure that women feel they are a valuable asset to the company.

Organic Growth

Organic growth focuses on expanding its revenue, employees, and location.[10] Organic growth is impressive and a good way to strengthen a company before external expansion options are considered. The process of organic growth focuses on managing and balancing the four pillars of company growth internally. If any of these pillars underperform or do not keep up with the other three posts, the company's growth structure will collapse.

Revenue

Revenue is the basis of any company's growth. If a company is not making a tangible profit every year, it is not on any growth track. It is not on any growth track on any growth track. Some business owners or C.E.O.s feel that they only have to show substantial numbers at the end

---

[10] Spolsky, Joel. 2008. "The Four Pillars of Organic Growth | How Hard Could It Be? By Joel Spolsky." *Inc.Com.* Retrieved from (https://www.inc.com/magazine/20080101/how-hard-could-it-be-the-four-pillars-of-organic-growth.html).

of the year, and then they can grow through external affiliations. The idea is not bad, but it will expose your company to external interference and chip away at your power one step at a time.

Until you are ready to sell your company, make sure that you do not enter into many joint ventures or partnerships that make your company unsuitable for a buyout. If you opt for organic growth, earning your revenue is only half the game. The rest of your efforts will fall into investing without involving external stakeholders. Expansion that focuses solely on production value is the best reward, but it also happens to be incredibly challenging.

You will enjoy a rollercoaster ride getting the fiscal growth against obstacles, seen and unseen. Even though the revenue you have generated looks high at that time, you will not find enough profit to invest in a complete unit. Then how will you create and expand your business?

The advantage of organic growth allows you to decide the pace to grow and utilize your resources without borrowing – to expand.

A smart strategy focuses on a core strategy to fuel organic growth to avoid pursuing multiple angles that may obscure your vision and plan. Start with identifying a target product or service and customer/client decision-makers you invite to be a part of the goal. Next, gather a team of employees to tailor a marketing plan and a target product or service towards customers who are your top buyers.

CHAPTER 11

PART 1-TARGET KPIS FOR GROWTH

KPIs are the backbone of modern and project management. KPIs are parameters used to gauge the success and failure of every project. Now that we have elaborated on the workforce and its prospects of growth, we should discuss KPIs and how they can be better evaluated.

Key Performance Indicators

Key Performance Indicators or KPIs are the metrics used by organizational management teams to evaluate an individual's success, a group, a department, or an organization in achieving the project goals. KPIs heavily rely on data and allow users to see their growth potential at the end of the quarter has to show [1].

Definition of a Metric

A metric in the KPI system is an activity or action that is measured according to a predesigned analysis markup. The markup can be a target, a benchmark, or a goal evaluated by allowing context. For example, if you look at your company's growth in a down economy, the numbers will likely be modest. But suppose you look at the same numbers with the economic stagnation across the spectrum. In that case, these are strong indicators to consider as most of the industries are impacted in a down economy, while few may find new opportunities.

Streamline your KPIs

You can streamline your Key Performance Indicators (KPIs) by allowing these simple rules to be a part of your project planning criteria:

If an action or activity directly affects the project's progress, it can only be counted as a KPI. Many stories or activities do not have either a negative or a positive effect on the KPI; these metrics should not be measured in the KPI evaluation.

KPIs need to be clearly defined. That is a challenge when most of the tasks are complex, but there has to be one final action or conclusion to be measured and evaluated against a target outcome.

All actions cannot be equally evaluated. One action has a profound impact, while another action has a minimal effect. There has to be impact metrics that work as a relative element in evaluation. Every activity should be evaluated and scored on a scale from 1 – 5 based on priority and scored to determine the relative impact and desired outcome.

Developing benchmarks can also be a challenge. To be obtainable, use SMART goals to measure results and achieve a milestone or completion of a phase to allow for the small victories to be counted and celebrated in the evaluation.

Outlining your KPIs

Following is a list of important steps for outlining the KPIs. The evaluation's basic idea focuses on the primary objective and indicator for success. If you can connect these two elements, you have a good head start. Here are four major requirements of the KPI outline. These are listed here:

Your Business Model

Your KPI will be heavily dependent on your business model. How do you define success in your business is dependent on your business objectives? For example, if you aim to get the word out and gain your customers' attention, this KPI will be different from generating revenue. These differences will change the KPI outline.

The Stage of Your Business

Whether you are a small business or a large enterprise, the lifecycle of a business includes (1) startup, (2) growth, (3) maturity, and (4) decline. If you are an entrepreneur, your KPIs will be completely different from a multinational conglomerate. KPIs vary drastically depending on the scope of success a company can expect. Depending on which of the four revenue cycle - expansion, prosperity, contraction, and recession – your business is in will also determine your KPIs. The company's size will undoubtedly play a significant role, but your revenue cycle will also define the KPIs you will decide for the company.

As an example, the following illustration outlines key result areas that make up a sample revenue cycle:

Using this example, the following information will illustrate the importance of decision-making supported by metrics and how to define and categorize KPIs.

Supporting Metrics

External market's economic trends, your business position in the target market, your team's capacity and capability, and many other similar factors are examples of supporting metrics. Knowing your supporting metrics, internally and externally, are important so that the company can capture impacting factors to be considered while they decide and create their KPI framework.

Few KPIs are Good KPIs

Be wise in deciding the number of KPIs - they cannot be a list of hundred metrics that your team needs to do and create a state of paralysis because the target goal seems daunting and out of reach. Instead, choose a method to categorize the KPIs into four buckets and categories. KPIs are not like a checklist but a methodology to control and measure key performance indicators to accomplish the business key result areas (KRAs).

Three Types of KPIs

There are three types of KPIs based on the unit of execution. These KPIs will be elaborated with examples in this section.

Business KPI

Business KPI is a major unit of performance measurement companies use. Business KPIs focus on its monthly revenue and performance to achieve the target goals. If the entire business has other target revenue goals, they can also be included in this bucket. You can mostly see that monthly recurring revenue is the leading business KPI.

Departmental KPI

A departmental KPI or team's KPI will contribute to the company goals. The first and foremost KPI will evaluate how much of the expected tasks did the team complete in the provided time frame. Did the team achieve its metrics, or are they lagging in achieving the expected targets?

Individual KPIs

The employees' KPIs focus on how the employees perform their tasks and achieve their goals. The KPIs are the basic unit of the KPI metric as they build-up to the departmental and business metrics. Individuals KPIs are usually assigned at the early stages of the quarter to evaluate individual performance for complete company assessment.

The following pyramid illustrates an example of how the three types of KPIs accomplish revenue goals:

Leaders and Lagers- Differences

A business's performance will heavily depend on the motivation that senior management provides to its employees. Here is a list of different management styles between leaders and lagers. Leaders motivate the employees to offer company growth while lagers push the employees into disengagement and exhaustion[2].

Vision vs. Goal

Most managers think that goals run the team. If you give the team a target and achieve the target, it is well done. That is far from the truth. The vision that you provide to your team will outlive the goals. Let's suppose you told your team to make X number of sales. They can either make the sales to meet the quota or see the value of increasing sales.

If you explain the sales target is to expand the business and increase their customers in the market, your team will be motivated to work hard. You can also incentivize them by showing how it is done and how their effort will also help you achieve departmental goals.

Change vs. Status Quo

The world is fast evolving, and as is the way to get a job done. Most managers become obsessed with procedures because they fear new ways to problem-solve. But the ever-changing world requires an open mind and a go-getter attitude. Allow your employees to try new ways to solve problems, and your team will grow exponentially.

Innovation vs. Not-So Unique

Innovation as a need contradicts the notion that every solution requires a solution. That is not the focus but to find original solutions that cater to the problem. Managers should have a tool belt of solutions that they offer for an issue at hand. The managers may also facilitate their team to innovate a solution closest to the problem.

A result that lacks innovation as part of the solution becomes a poorly fitting glove that does not fully solve it. The answer is that companies should encourage managers to find innovative ideas as solutions to major problems that impact the business key result areas.

Risk Takers Vs. Risk Controllers

Risks are a part of business management, and those who avoid risks always stay small. If you want to grow, you have to be open to risk-taking. Risk-taking does not mean going out of your way to take risks but an art of critical thinking to take *calculated risks*. Some problems require you to think outside of the lines to find solutions that need impactful results.

Risks are always going to occur. But rather than being controlled by the risk, take on the challenges that run your business to be risk-averse. That will allow you to have more robust control over your expertise, and you will strengthen your position. It is also an excellent way to push your KPI towards growth.

Longer-Term Vs. Short-Term Vision

According to Forbes[11], long-term vision is why Robert Smith, the founder of Vista Equity Partners, has become America's fastest-growing private equity firm, managing $31 billion across a range of buyout, credit, and hedge funds. Those who believe in the brand and product invest in ways that do not make much short-sighted sense but are an excellent way for the company to thrive.

---

[11] Vardi, Nathan. n.d. "Richer Than Oprah: How The Nation's Wealthiest African-American Conquered Tech And Wall Street." *Forbes*. Retrieved from (https://www.forbes.com/sites/nathanvardi/2018/03/06/richer-than-oprah-how-the-nations-wealthiest-african-american-conquered-tech-and-wall-street/).

Those who believe in short term goals and successes avoid any investments that cannot be justified in the next three months. These individuals have perfect yearly reports but never any creativity or leaps of faith to report. They are usually never considered to join the summit.

Personal Vs. Professional Mentorship

Mentorship is a prerequisite for all business owners, C.E.O.s, and entrepreneurs. You are expected to mentor your employees and leaders, but what kind of mentorship are you offering? Are you always pushing your team to work hard and never consider their wellbeing? That is not mentorship; mentorship is a relationship where you make your employee your priority. Their wellbeing and health matters to you. You are invested in their growth and career path, and you take it as your responsibility to ensure their experience with the company.

These few tips will help you and your leaders to breed a healthier workforce. The power of a brand lies in your human capital. If workers believe in the company, they become more productive. Their performance enhances, and they deliver strong and viable results.

Account Payable Rate Management Tips

Accounts payable will make or break the company. The money a company owes to its employees, vendors, and other stakeholders are the company's most significant liability to manage. Here are a few simple ways for you to improve your company's account payable process:

Early Start

Like any other financial transaction, an early start of getting through the balance sheet will help in promising results. Always start invoice approval early and not wait for the deadline. A company has to pay a long list of invoices. If the company approves the invoices early and timely, they get more time to research and backcheck every invoice before payment.

If a finance department processes all the invoices early, they do not have to ensure any late payment penalties, and they may be eligible for early payment discounts. Most importantly, it makes for a good reputation in the market when your brand has an identity for fiscal responsibility.

References

[1] Anon. 2021. "How to Choose KPIs That Inspire Action." *Geckoboard Blog*. Retrieved from (https://www.geckoboard.com/blog/defining-kpis-how-to-choose-metrics-that-inspire-action/).

[2] Arruda, William. n.d. "9 Differences Between Being A Leader And A Manager." *Forbes*. Retrieved from (https://www.forbes.com/sites/williamarruda/2016/11/15/9-differences-between-being-a-leader-and-a-manager/).

CHAPTER 11

PART 2-UNDERSTANDING OF KPIS THROUGH A CASE STUDY

This case study will examine Unilever's Lipton Tea distribution expansion due to acquiring certified tea for international locations under new management. In this chapter, I will share the phenomenon and process of managing change and the Lipton Tea evolution under a new government and discuss various management types at the organizational level. This chapter will conclude with change management strategies that tie to achieving several key performance indicators (KPIs) suitable for this global company and recommendations to Unilever based on several findings.

Change Management and Leadership

There are many types and approaches to conduct organizational and leadership change. A few of these are as follows:

Burke-Litwin model

Burke-Litwin's[12] organizational model focuses on the correlation between transactional and transformational relationships in the

---

[12] "Burke-Litwin: The Performance and Change Model." Retrieved from (https://www.accipio.com/eleadership/mod/wiki/view.php?id=1848).

organization. For example, the organizational climate is a transactional factor. The primary model focuses on the twelve elements that affect the dynamics of change in an organization. The focus is on understanding the factors that are easy to change, as opposed to the harder ones. The analysis allows the C.E.O. or business owner to choose whether to focus on large organizational change measures to counteract the small or minor organizational changes that can impact corporate direction.

ADKAR model

The Prosci research center developed the ADKAR framework[13] of understanding and executing change at the organizational level by starting the transformation with leadership, followed by getting employees to buy-in and adopt organizational changes and aligning their behaviors for successful execution. Transformation of the organization is best achieved by changing individual and team behavior to impact organizational change successfully. The ADKAR model has five elements that derive the change model. Those five elements are as follows; change engagement through participation, the essential requirements of change, the power to implement the difference, and strengthening the growth through policy.

These two organizational change approaches offer essential steps for change management and ensure that the transformation practices are useful in the long term for sustaining a new system that is a major challenge in accomplishing organizational change.

---

[13] Inc, Prosci. n.d. "ADKAR Change Management Model Overview | Prosci." Retrieved from (https://www.prosci.com/adkar/adkar-model).

Unilever

Unilever is a multinational conglomerate with the most prestigious production system for tea products used in ordinary day to day life. The company has operations on all continents and has manufacturing and distribution operations in nearly 200 countries worldwide. The company appointed a new brand development director Michael Linjse[14] whose management portfolio included a professional mission to refresh the famous Lipton brand. The product is already an established brand with a strong marketing apparatus in play. The director conducted the requisite research and concluded that the company could significantly enhance the brand position and stature if their tea products were grown and harvested by certified plantations. The executive team approved the idea, and the project operations commenced. The search for certified third-party tea-producing farms was initiated, and Rainforest Alliance, Inc., a US-based non-profit biodiversity organization known for its collective strategies between people and nature, helped solidify Linjse's vision. They were also chosen for their data-inform certification and credentials. The global operations were aligned through third party associations with local industries to ensure that the certification requirements were met on a country-by-country basis. The results of the change initiative were successful. As a key result, the Lipton brand grew more successful worldwide and became more famous with younger populations through the initiatives.

The Risk

The risk for Michael Linjse's initiative was that every country has its own agriculture requirements for different markets, legal and farming

---

[14] Anon. n.d. "Sign Up | LinkedIn." Retrieved from https://www.linkedin.com/in/michael-lenson-88364b53

rules, and regulations. To sync all of these diverse agricultural rules and regulations, the initiative involved developing a uniform standard for global tea production, which led to eligibility requirements for a legitimate certification based on a unique set of requirements and procedures that allowed for methods exclusively for each country. Once all the farms were aligned, the promotion and marketing became more successful.

Key Points

Following are the key points to consider from this case study:

a. The organizational change theory and understanding the various aspects of the organizational change requires a case-by-case evaluation.

b. The execution of organizational change includes a practical basis and examining the issues in these plans.

c. The issues that occur in organizational change execution and how to counteract them involve practical solutions. Top management that could assist in the organizational change is imperative to ensure that the plans are executed to the project's requirement.

Content and Analysis

In this section, Unilever's organizational plan to improve its structure to execute the change initiative included a series of evaluations to ensure that the organizational change was realistically feasible. Here, in this section, Unilever's case study offers more important details for further evaluation.

1) <u>External Factors:</u> Unilever's main issue was internal organizational factors and consideration for a wide range of external factors that had to be dealt with to ensure that the project was executed successfully.

2) <u>Legal Issues:</u> Every country has its legal framework that requires different execution for each farmland. The process is enormous and required an extensive understanding of the local legal framework.[15]

3) <u>Farming Culture:</u> The certification required the execution of a long list of human rights and worker rights regulations that are new to many countries. Tea is specially grown in Africa, where human rights execution is a complex local issue and had to be dealt with separately.

4) <u>Certification Guidelines:</u> The certification guidelines had to be upheld accurately, and that could be challenging when the farming operations are spread in a wide net. That is why the process required extensive review and deference.

Internal Factors

Various internal operations were also greatly affected by the execution of the plan. A few are as follows:

1) <u>Quality Assurance:</u> The certification requires a high degree of quality assurance that is not guaranteed in every farmland. The company had to ensure that the local farmers followed the initiative's certification guidelines.

---

[15] Taylor. 2018. "Common Farm Law Issues Tip Sheets." *Beginning Farmers*. Retrieved from (https://www.beginningfarmers.org/common-farm-law-issues-tip-sheets/).

2) <u>Third-Party Assistance:</u> every branch involved in the project had to find a third-party partner who would help execute the certification requirements in every farmland to enforce and implement these guidelines locally. This was not a minor task. The assessment of third-party partners is a challenging task, as well.

3) <u>Barriers to Change:</u> The reason for the change initiative was to implement an approved standardized certification process to work in collaboration with many countries around the world. Following are barrier factors that could affect the change process:

4) <u>Internal Organization:</u> The international standard of farming is a strict criterion to achieve. Many cultures have agriculture standards that are age-old traditions that are virtually not exposed to modern standards. The process has led to a great wave of need to develop and implement awareness quickly that is not practically easy to achieve. And yet, the time frame for execution demands that the process is executed successfully.

5) <u>Third-Party Association:</u> Third-party association in third world countries can be hesitant because institutional stability is atypical in some tea producing countries. To find the correct partner to execute the project, the company had to develop a process that evaluated the presented options in finding a suitable partner. If the partnerships fail, they will affect the execution of the process, and to ensure that the partnerships sustain, the companies require careful evaluation.[16]

---

[16] Evans, Michael. "10 Key Steps To Expanding Your Business Globally." *Forbes*. Retrieved from(https://www.forbes.com/sites/allbusiness/2015/03/04/10-key-steps-to-expanding-your-business-globally/).

External Factors

Various external factors also affected the process of developing eligible certified tea farmlands. A few external factors were considered (Oreg & Berson; pg. 630).

1) <u>Farmlands:</u> The local farmers and their farmlands are extensively diverse depending on the country. In some states, the laws and regulations are exceptionally different and to develop farmlands that will pass the certification requires extensive agriculture lobbying in the government. The certification was an intense complexity because the process is strenuous.

2) <u>Local Regulations:</u> Every country has its regulations that change frequently. With changes in laws, every country's land will have to be readjusted to continue upholding the rules. That is why executing the process was in danger of unnecessary hurdles and problems.

Change Implementation

Unilever's change implementation was extensive, and the type of change implemented by Unilever cannot be justified as a conventional approach. The approach can be described as a customized plan that focused on choosing third-party partnerships for every country and ensuring that every country followed the rules individually. The strategies that were implemented are as follows:

1) <u>Individual Execution:</u> Here, the basic concept of ADRAK is that individual behavior has to be improved to support an organization's system's performance. The company developed a system that requires every country's evaluation on a case-by-case basis. It ensured that each case execution was performing to

support the initiative. The method involved developing the culture in every branch of the distribution chain. It also ensured that no country would be lost in the clusters that usually hide weaker cases.

2) <u>Thorough Implementation:</u> If a company had not formed an affiliation with an international certification body, the results might not have been that well-formed. The fact that a company had to demonstrate its accountability system and allow an external entity to monitor its internal systems and allow the world to show that a company could choose accountability.[17]

3) <u>Serious Execution:</u> The process of evaluating each company and the management of every country is an arduous task and is one of the most challenging parts of a certification initiative. But the certification process also ensured that the process was extensive and allowed the company to demonstrate that the change was uniformly implemented. The process was also extensively challenging for brand management because they had to deal with many diverse farmlands. The certification process also allowed for strict and direct accountability.

4) <u>Initiative:</u> These extensive processes are usually considered when a company is a profitable business, there is an opportunity to expand the brand, or the company wants to reclaim a more competitive position. Even though the task of elevating the brand was at hand, could the target have been achieved from a minor marketing campaign of rebranding? In this instance,

---

[17] velocityglobal. 2019. "Top 5 Global Expansion Strategies." *Velocity Global*. Retrieved from (https://velocityglobal.com/blog/top-5-global-expansion-strategies/).

Unilever chose to evolve their entire operation globally without any prompting from external initiatives because they believed that the timing was right for their industry. This initiative attitude is why the process was admired globally, and other companies also had to follow suit (Fletcher; pg. 650).

Leadership Theories

Many leadership theories can be utilized to understand and manage worker resistance issues. Many leadership theorists could have studied Unilever when they hired Michael Linjse, who disrupted the status quo by implementing certification standards for tea producing countries and distributors. A few types of leadership practices that could have helped to prepare for the change are as follows:

1) **The natural leader:** The natural leader is a type that individuals follow without prompting. These kinds of leaders are a great asset in dealing with employee resistance issues because workers usually trust them. They guide their teams towards success and are instrumental in gaining significant progress in the process.

2) **Leadership by participation:** When a leader becomes a part of the process, the process improves greatly. Leading by example works because it diminishes the worker's perceptions or beliefs that the company has unfair practices. If their bosses are also following the same working conditions themselves, it is hard to point the finger at the management.

3) **Leadership by reward/punishment:** This is the most ill-advised form of organizational management because it encourages management to motivate employees through fear and encourages leadership reward incentives based on fear and greed.

The incentive-based motivation practice is most common in the workplace, but it is a culture that requires a set of values that are based on respect and treating employees with dignity.

4) **<u>Motivational Leadership:</u>** Motivation leadership asks that the leader motivates her team to complete the projects through understanding and motivation. This style of leadership requires the ability to influence and inspired employees. The leadership style is based on the leader who feels connected to her employees and motivates them through effective communication.

In conclusion, the certification of tea farms that provide the tea to Lipton was a groundbreaking action that increased worker rights awareness worldwide. The companies worldwide observed while Unilever executed a complex and highly demanding initiative that was not easy to implement. The process required that the company develop a strong sense of worker awareness and an execution strategy deeply rooted in corporate responsibility. The plan was executed in 1996, and it required all the competitors to develop similar cultures focused on worker safety and sustainability.

Following are a few recommendations for companies who wish to become socially responsible companies to follow:

#1: The worker health and benefit plans should be implemented by all companies with a similar zeal and zest. Corporate responsibility initiatives are usually seen as superficial because they do not directly improve company revenue. But this is factually not true. These initiatives allow the company to ensure that employee welfare and quality of life programs also develop and support its infrastructure. The company will benefit from such an initiative socially and are often sustainable for the long run. The world has continued to grow, and those companies who do not develop employee welfare and qualify of life benefits their shortsightedness will impact their brand and growth opportunities.

#2: Execution of plans should consider the scope of the company's challenges. Unilever considered and developed a thorough plan for certification standards and regulations required for the program's execution. Their process included local cultures and ensured that the local systems were considered. Unilever's success took into account the various issues occurring in every country exclusive of each other. These issues could not be dealt with globally and understood locally. That is why their plan included the solutions that were considerate of the local farming cultures.

Unilever has been the pioneer of taking local cultures into account. The company has a policy of entering into the country's market as if they belong. The entire workforce ethic and work ethic are developed carefully to allow the company workers to feel that they are a part of the company. Once the company has seen that it has settled into the region, they implemented international standards to the local culture. Unilever is attributed to providing global quality to local products worldwide.

You will enjoy a roller coastal ride getting the fiscal growth against obstacles, seen and unseen. Even though the revenue you have generated looks high at that time, you will not find enough profit to invest in a complete unit. Then how will you create and expand your business?

The advantage of organic growth allows you to decide the pace to grow and utilize your resources without borrowing – to expand.

A smart strategy focuses on a core strategy to fuel organic growth to avoid pursuing multiple angles that may obscure your vision and plan. Start with identifying a target product or service and customer/client decision-makers you invite to be a part of the goal. Next, gather a team of employees to tailor a marketing plan and a target product or service towards customers who are your top buyers.

CHAPTER 12

PART1- MAKING TOUGH DECISIONS FOR GROWTH

Tough decision making about your company is the focus of this chapter. The business world thrives on creativity and innovation, and small businesses have to follow suit. The growth and expansion of modern business require creativity and tough decision making in strategy and execution. The social and organizational structures invented fifty years ago have become outdated with modern creativity and innovation. Entrepreneurs and business owners must consider developing a creative workplace and enhance a leadership style that encourages innovation.

The Dhofar Automotive Company Case Study for Growth Based Decisions

In this case study, the Dhofar Automotive Company will be analyzed for its challenges in setting a path for organizational growth. The company struggles with defining a leadership development approach to prepare the entire organization to embrace innovation. This case study will highlight an organizational development plan that will focus on talent, creativity, and design that will push all the employees from top to bottom towards embracing and using a creative mindset to support organizational growth.

Why Is Growth Important?

The case study begins with the significance of growth for its success. The case study and research outlined the complications and hurdles that creativity and innovation may face and how to counteract these problems. The case study's objective is to highlight employee creativity through modern methods to improve organizational performance.

The need for small businesses to understand the competitive nature of growth is significant because the competition grows stronger over time, and it is always in motion. Creativity and innovation have come to the forefront of modern debate, and performance focuses on ensuring the results desired cannot be completed using outdated conventional methods.[18]

The competitive advantage and market position of a company heavily depends on its potential to manage its organizational structure's growth and expansion. The expansion and brand recognition of a company and its products and services are heavily dependent upon the company's growth.

The problems in achieving these goals are limited by communication, outdated policies and procedures, an outdated viewpoint, and a rigid organizational structure built upon antiquated perceptions and mindsets. The Dhofar Automotive Company has adapted thoroughly to the modern requirements for growth.[19]

---

[18] Bass, B.M. and Avolio, B.J., 1993. Transformational leadership: A response to critiques.
[19] Ekvall, G., 1997. Organizational conditions and levels of creativity. *Creativity and innovation Management*, 6(4), pp.195-205.

Understand Creativity to Understand Growth:

The EOI model (Environment Organization Individual) was considered for creativity models to offer an example of how an organization can conduct highly creative and innovative workplace sessions. The format provides an essential outline for launching the creativity and innovation model with an individual or group. External factors such as stakeholders, executives, and board members are all considered a possible barrier to creativity and innovation.

The barriers may come via employees' development in creativity and innovation. These hurdles can be found in The Dhofar Automotive organizational structure and why EOI was used to understand the challenges and barriers to achieve the goals. The company was built on antiquated models that were traditional and yet outdated. The work policies were constricted and limited in their scope of execution.

Train Your Employees

The company's commitment to employees' training was limited and not adequately fulfilled. These barriers showed significant limitations in the growth process of an organization.[20]

The Ekvall Solution

Goran Ekvall pioneered creativity in the organization in his research. His process of enhancing creativity and innovation in the organization begins with a questionnaire that focuses on building creativity and innovation.

The Ekvall questionnaire was ideal for developing the plan's outline that The Dhofar Automotive Company followed to enhance creativity

---

[20] Ekvall, G., 1999. Creative climate. *Encyclopedia of creativity*, *1*, pp.403-412.

and innovation. The analysis conducted for this discussion showed that its organizational system was not appropriate for the EOI creativity and innovation model (Isaksen, Lauer, & Ekvall, page. 170).

In an organizational setting, the business and cultural design should understand constrictions, limiting creativity and innovation. The problems such as cultural misalignment can perpetuate a restricted mindset and antiquated perspectives. When combined with discouragement and restrictive communication, the combination will hinder creative thought development.

These issues can be altered by changing the leadership strategy in the company. A company's leadership can define innovation and creativity and breaks through unrealistic attachment to hierarchies and organizational structure.

With changing times, the modern environment of Dhofar Automotive needed change with their leadership strategy to lead to innovation and change. Despite the effort to embrace creativity and innovation, the workforce does not feel that the company welcomed change and innovation.

The Evolution Journey

As the Dhofar Automotive Company's evaluation shows, the cultural and structural barriers to growth highlighted power distribution in the workplace. The leadership had to allow the employees to develop new ideas to perform and creatively break through the problems.

The leadership model that was ideal for The Dhofar Automotive Company is the transformational leadership model that enhanced the workforce's creativity and innovation. Active participation in the creativity strategy should be rewarded with remunerations and incentives to encourage workers to participate in the innovation strategy. The process allowed the employees to develop a critical interest in growth.

Play with Incentives

For example, incentives such as paid family trips, bonuses, medical allowance, or upgrade in the present medical insurance and other similar incentives encourage performance for personal reasons. This leadership strategy will enhance innovation and motivate the employees to engage in creativity. The primary issue with employees is that they felt disengaged with the culture and feel that their ideas will not be appreciated.

The RBV model (resource-based view) is a powerful tool to understand the human resource department's role in increasing the organization's creativity and innovation threshold and reducing barriers to these motivational and creative perspectives. The model focuses on developing an organizational structure that focuses on a healthier workspace (Ekval; pg.200).[21]

The human resource management at The Dhofar Automotive Company was not optimal in its execution of modern human resource practices. Most of the company's issues in recent years were simply a result of poor human resource practices.

The RBV model will ensure that the company will develop a strong human resource management strategy that will result in its successful transformation. The company also found the process new and unfamiliar

---

[21] Ekvall, G., 1996. Organizational climate for creativity and innovation. European journal of work and organizational psychology, 5(1), pp.105-123.

because it had to change its mindset and become more competitive in the global market.

Solution

This case study was focused on innovative and creative ways essential for an organization's growth. It has become the cornerstone of success in the modern business world. The business world encounters various problematic issues in an ever-changing global market, changing governmental policies, fluctuating economies, and evolving trends; small business owners find themselves in unprecedented battles daily.

Out of the Box Thinking

These tasks and challenges cannot be dealt with unless the company is willing to connect with creative and out of the box thinking.

As many examples have exhibited throughout the book, multiple theories exist that can elaborate on the necessity for creativity and innovation. Various models have been developed that focus on developing creativity and innovation in the workplace. The models are all developed through thorough evaluation and understanding of the main theories.

But the main issue at The Dhofar Automotive Company was the antiquated leadership practice that was driving the company into a harmful pitfall. The RBV model is significant as it allows the human resource department to become more connected with creativity and innovation. If the human resource department develops a stronger focus on human resource management systems, it will solve many fundamental problems (Isaksen & Ekvall; pg.80).

Things You Should Try

Following are the recommendations offered to enhance the creativity and innovation mindset in The Dhofar Automotive Company:

The leadership strategy is the critical factor in bringing permanent change. Management must increase its engagement with a problem-solving mindset. Many managers and executives develop tunnel vision in these settings and believe that their knowledge is superior to others.

In this case study, the EOI model and the transformational leadership model were suggested here because the models focused on changing executives' mindset and leadership. Their changed perspective can lead to a change in the employees' mindset.

The strategic implementing style should focus on designing a good process that focuses on employees conducting their work with a creative and innovative mindset. Creativity and innovation ensure that the change is permanent and comes from the roots.

The Ekvall questionnaire is a significant process to enhance the workforce's strength and develop a consistent innovative perspective.

The questionnaire and module also focus on evaluating effective innovative and creative strategies. The climate of creativity essential to building the company will be garnered through these practices.

The growth threshold is best served by new managers who believe in the idea. If the managerial staff feels forced to implement a free and communicative policy without belief, it will agonize them. Best to develop the managerial staff for open communication policy from the get-go.

All in all, tough decisions require creativity and flexibility of perspective. You cannot find practical solutions to everyday workplace issues with a closed mindset. Have an agile and curious view and try creative techniques to find reasonable solutions to everyday problems.

CHAPTER 12

PART 2-MAKING TOUGH DECISIONS FOR GROWTH

One of my clients is a federal contractor and supplies door and window products. Their business model was heavily wrapped around customer service and customer satisfaction. They wanted their HR policies to be developed to enhance the employee's ability to work best with the customers and provide exceptional customer service.

The HR strategic direction employed employee-centered policies to enhance customer care under their 'People' value statement; "To attract and retain innovative, customer-focused employees who can support our expanding business, and reward performance fairly and equitably."

As the statement suggests, the main aim was to foster well-being and growth-oriented work culture among employees. The HR policies' main objectives were to be transparent and accountable. Following is a summary of findings:

The employees are evaluated every six months to communicate their performance. They also received informal coaching from their supervisors.

In case of performance issues, the employee was notified immediately, and feedback is offered to improve.

In terms of performance enhancement, programs such as personality assessments and coaching were offered to improve performance and awareness of strengths.

These tools and resources are intended to outline the importance of understanding and evaluating employee performance to measure how their performance impacted customer satisfaction. However, the business strategy lacked a focus on employee skill enhancement through various initiatives.

Recommended Changes

As much as my client wanted to implement HR policies and procedures to enhance customer services, their policies emphasized policies and training for managers to use and reinforce the tools and resources available to the employees. Some managers provided informal coaching and feedback, but this practice was not uninformed among all managers.

To address this inconsistency, a reference manual was developed as a tool to define further the supervisory role in retaining innovative, customer-focused employees. The manual was also a tool to expand business strategies and guidelines for rewarding performance fairly and equitably. Frequently communicating changing performance needs to be measured and tracked key result areas were also a part of the customer satisfaction initiative.

Findings from this business need suggest that a uniform approach to providing supervisory support, tools, and frequent communication helped employees deliver much better performance to improve customer satisfaction. The recommendation shifts the focus from the employee's performance to the manager's performance and supervisors. The role of supervisors and managers is vital in a customer-oriented business. The understanding that the customer experience is linked to employee performance is shaped by HR policies and practices that support the business goals and performance outcomes.

Today's research shows us that employee performance is linked to business outcomes and shepherd by managers and supervisors to account for target outcomes. As much as employees' accountability is important, establishing rapport with them and earning their loyalty is essential for running a successful business unit.

More Steps to Improve HR Management

As suggested earlier, developing a company culture where supervisors focused more on retaining highly talented employees is imperative to their goal. Following are steps recommended to enhance further the HR strategic direction employed for employee-centered policies to achieve customer care under their 'People' value statement:

- Provide the supervisors with special training to learn about customer-centered culture and innovation flexibility that focus on result-oriented behavior.

- Provide managers with behavioral training to provide guidance and coaching to boost employee engagement.

A comprehensive approach should involve enhanced HR policies and practices that enrich the organization through building capability and capacity to achieve business goals.

The Strategic Plan for Enhancing Employee Relations

Employee Relations Plan

An employee relations plan should consider the recommendations mentioned and a strategic plan that adheres to employee growth instead of employee accountability. Following are the steps to consider in developing an employee relations plan:

Active listening

The workplace should develop values where supervisors feel it is their responsibility to cultivate and mentor their employees rather than pursue pointless evaluations.

Inclusivity

Promote an approach that encourages weekly team meetings and conversations where all team members come together with their supervisors to discuss wins, losses, and innovation to improve performance. These group discussions can disclose gaps and problems that employees may be experiencing in their work and inviting diverse thinking to solve problems. Team meetings are also a great way to help relieve tension and help teams brainstorm to develop productive solutions to new workplace problems.

Timing

Group exercises help enhance the employee's trust among each other and with their supervisor. Strong collaboration among the team is key to effective team performance. Employees would benefit from understanding how to see their work in the greater context of helping their local community. Supervisors should strive to give meaning to their work that makes an employee feel like they are moving in the right direction and contributing to their local communities in a meaningful way.

Commit to your decision

Team building should be enhanced by using forward-thinking techniques and facilitation to bridge differences and highlight group similarities to promote diverse thinking styles. Team building outdoor experiences are also great to develop camaraderie among employees who are expected to deliver results interdependently.

Psychological Profiling of the Employees

Psychological evaluations may be an option for hiring employees. HR professionals and business owners are encouraged to understand employment law for using testing and assessments as a condition of employment. Post-hire, personality, or strength-based assessments help understand the employee's strengths, limitations, and strategies to mitigate limited areas. These assessments should focus more on understanding the employee's personality and information crucial to helping the new team member fit with their new team.

Personality conflict

Personality assessments can guide the HR professional to help supervisors facilitate a new team member's onboarding. Employees should be placed to utilize their strengths and are not forced to struggle with their weaknesses unnecessarily. The HR department should also advise supervisors to explain how to help the new employee adapt and meet performance goals. Support for the supervisor will feel like HR is designed to help him run the team.

Cliques

As these programs are implemented, a shift in power structure occurs. This gives rise to a few problems that the HR department will have to resolve. There are a few possible deviations that one can foresee:

Lack of Compatibility

Perhaps there is a possible lack of compatibility in placement strategy as there are no perfect places for the employees. But the HR department should ensure that at least the employee is allowed to work to their strengths.

Lack of Harmony

If there are compatibility issues between a supervisor and an employee, HR policies and practices should allow the employee to ask for a change without any social retribution.

Mindset Limitations

Supervisors should not consider the newly implemented teambuilding exercises and group sessions as unnecessary and losing the power structure. These are typical concerns when new policies and changes are implemented in any business. The role of HR is to ensure that these practices support management and are executed without acts of sabotage.

References

Salanova, Marisa, et al. "Linking Organizational Resources and Work Engagement to Employee Performance and Customer Loyalty: The Mediation of Service Climate." Journal of Applied Psychology, vol. 90, no. 6, 2005, pp. 1217–1227., doi:10.1037/0021-9010.90.6.1217.

Ulrich, Dave, et al. "Human resource competencies: An empirical assessment." Human resource management 34.4 (1995): 473-495.

CHAPTER 13

BENCHMARKING THE GROWTH

Growth is the aim of every company when they begin their journey forward. From franchising to organic expansion, companies either grow or shrink. They rarely remain stagnant. But how do you effectively grow and effectively manage your business expansion issues? Here is Radio One's example, as they went through a diversification process.

Following a merger, Clear Channel wanted a divestiture of a number of its radio stations. Radio One (NYSE: ROIA and RIOAK), the largest radio group targeting African-Americans in the country, had achieved tremendous success through acquiring the underperforming radio stations and using their skills like programming, marketing, and effective operations to cut the cost and making those stations work better.

Radio One acquisition of the 12 established urban stations in the top 50 markets doubled the company's size and would also help build its national platform.

These radio stations were from the top fifty markets within the US, and they represented a significant growth opportunity for Radio One.

They estimated the projected after-tax cash flows from the new station. They then used the appropriate discount rate to value the new radio stations using a discounted cash flow approach. This approach's value is also substantiated by employing an independent multiple-based valuation. In the end, the values derived from these approaches are compared to suggest an appropriate acquisition price for the radio channels.

The Classic Benchmarks

Radio One was faced with a rare opportunity to grow through multiple radio station acquisitions in the top fifty markets. The window of opportunity was due to Clear Channel's impending divestiture of radio stations. The divestiture provided Radio One's opportunity to acquire twelve urban stations located in the US's top fifty African-American markets. Even though the company had grown tremendously through acquisitions over the past decade, this situation was unique and could increase the company's market dominance to a significant extent. The company was also considering nine other stations in separate transactions. These cumulative transactions would double the company's size and give it a national presence in the African-American market.

The acquisitions were expected to create a more extensive advertising base geared towards African-American than any other media corporation in the US. Furthermore, the African-American population segment was growing at a higher rate. Their incomes were increasing at a significantly higher rate compared to the population and income growth of other average Americans. These factors were likely to result in significant revenues for Radio One following the acquisitions. The acquisitions would also result in cost-savings through economies of scale, reduction of duplicate staffing, and programming syndication. However, it was understood that certain risks were involved with the acquisitions.

This acquisition was a large transaction that would result in a drastic increase in its size. The acquisitions would double the number of radio stations controlled by Radio One, increasing operations' complexity. The management's inability to cope with these changes could lead to inefficiency and losses. Moreover, since the company recently engaged in an IPO transaction, it might have had to arrange further capital through debt financing, which would have raised its leverage ratios. Nevertheless, if the management was confident about its ability to handle larger size effectively, the acquisitions promised to augment significant value for its shareholders.

Impact of Cash flow Projections on Business Expansion

The broadcast cash flow projections from the new radio stations represented a greater proportion of the total projected broadcast cash flows of Radio One. Since the number of new stations was approximately equal to that of the company's existing stations, the new stations' cash projections were higher because they were over-estimated. However, the new stations were based in the top fifty African-Americans markets. Therefore, it was realistic to assume that advertisers would be willing to pay more for these markets, and revenues from new markets were expected to be higher than the revenues from existing markets. Nevertheless, the new stations' projected cash flows represented a considerable portion of the total cash flows. Any miscalculations could have grave consequences for the company's total value. Therefore, caution was exercised in estimating these cash flows.

The After-Tax Cash Flows

The after-tax cash flows were calculated by adjusting the broadcast cash flows for additional items that affected income. These subsequent calculations were shown as net broadcast cash flows (BCF) in the case study. The earnings before interest, taxes, depreciation, and amortization (EBITDA) were calculated by subtracting corporate expenses from BCF. The company's total corporate expenditures were allocated to the new stations with net BCF as the allocation base.

The earnings before interest and taxes (EBIT) were obtained by deducting depreciation and amortization from EBITDA. It was mentioned in the case study that the depreciation and amortization for the new stations amounted to $90 million. After-tax (NOPAT), the net operating profit was obtained by adjusting the EBIT for taxes. In the absence of any conclusive information, it was assumed that the effective tax rate for Radio One was 35% – the statutory corporate tax rate in the United States.

Planning for Benchmarking and Growth

The case study offered a deep dive into risk factors when Radio One decided to acquire the twelve stations from Clear Channel. Considerations for the acquisition included the following key points:

- Determining and assessing potential growth strategies in a target market

- Prioritizing best strategies based on an evaluation of current assets, cash flow, and leadership capabilities against a set of standards

- Identifying benchmarks and control standards

- Identifying cash flow to finance the needs of the acquisition

- Building out an acquisition strategy to manage capital spent and capital gains

One of the key things that stood out in the acquisition strategy was that Radio One's cost-cutting expertise helped make all 12 stations cut costs to earn more cash inflows. These centralized strategies also helped create synergies, which also helped the radio stations become more cost-efficient.

A major risk involved in acquiring these 12 stations would mean that the deal's size was huge and could create difficulties in managing these stations' integration.

A second risk was the acquisition benefits could have been undermined due to the cannibalization from existing listeners. Could the listeners of the already acquired radio stations get affected due to the large number of radio station company Radio One now held?

Another significant risk in the acquisition was the lack of expertise in the other media industries such as cable, recording, and internet realized from the acquisition and new channel opportunities.

Lessons Learned for Successful Benchmarking to Grow

Take-aways from this case study that may benefit a business positioning its growth strategies:

- Start with building a corporate level strategy – organize your findings and recommendations to answer the strategic business objectives. Your corporate strategy starts with analyzing its vision, mission, and key goals and how your strategy will take the company to the next level.

- Break down the department's growth strategy and how their solutions align with the corporate level strategy. Instead of providing recommendations for the overall company, each department or function breaks the strategy or function to avoid the contradiction of the company's overall growth strategy. For example, the corporate strategy can recommend low-cost solutions, but its core competency is creating custom solutions.

- Step away to clear your mind when you review your strategy. Invite your leadership team and independent critics to dissect your plan for gaps and inconsistencies.

- Be very deliberate with this process because rushing through the plan could lead to costly mistakes.

Hidden Risks of Benchmarking for Growth

According to the Chronicle Article, in the late 1970s, Xerox became the first major U.S. corporation to benchmark. The company analyzed all of its vital business functions and then compared the analysis to similar counterparts in other companies worldwide. Benchmarking eventually became a way to measure performance for companies of all sizes. Despite its many benefits for assessing performance, improving operations, and developing strategy, benchmarking has some inherent dangers that businesses must be considered.

Internal Versus External Benchmarking

Internal benchmarking is limited to gathering data from key departments within an organization and comparing them.

On the other hand, external benchmarking is like what Xerox did: they compared the company's overall performance to that of their competitors. When a company is confused by these two approaches, the results from information gathered through the benchmarking process will be convoluted in rendering useful results.

Resistance to Change

While benchmarking can help an organization develop plans for service improvement, product innovation, and design advancement, a major risk to the organization is with employees and managers who resist change and refuse to adopt the proposed changes. According to ADKAR, people resist change when they perceive the change will disrupt their daily routine, upsetting the learned workflow of how they accomplish their work. While this resistance can be managed, a greater danger is for the people who are participating in the benchmarking process will resist change and default to insisting that the company is performing to achieve the strategic goals, even if the data says otherwise.

Maintaining the Status Quo

When a company gathers useful data from the benchmarking process, it may decide whether it is best in the industry and decide to rest on its laurels. Benchmarking is not meant to lead to complacency but an opportunity to challenge ways to up their game and provide better customer service.

An organization that decides to grow must be willing to push the edges if they plan to expand or dominate their market. Thinking outside the box is extremely beneficial if you can combine benchmarked data with original and strategic innovation.

CHAPTER 14

BREAKTHROUGH FOR GROWTH

You Can Play BIG!

As I wrap up the last chapter, this book shares big ideas to step out of our small stories and use the strategies to step into extraordinary opportunities to grow. The successful case studies outlined how the companies did it, but they also identified some similarities. A few common themes among all of them are:

1. The status quo is the demise of creativity and innovation.
2. Whether big or small, the brand builds the message.
3. Customer service and sales drive revenue.
4. People, processes, and communication are essential to building engagement and productivity.
5. Knowing your market and competitors are winning advantages.
6. Good data and systems are imperative in planning or changing the strategy.
7. The CEO or business owner is the decision making, energy and involvement is the force that drives performance.
8. Personal brand, sway, and influence are in the *grit*.

9. Solutions are scalable.
10. A bottleneck is a pause but not a reason to derail a great opportunity.

How does a $100k company become a $million company, and how does a $million company become a $$billion company? It takes a BOSS attitude—amazing personal power, an unusual ability to turn insights, inspiration, and intentions into reality, and they build competitive teams.

These themes are also breakthroughs. I started this book defining BOSS:

They know how to get what
Live by a code of integrity
Have their own personality
They do not settle for less
A BOSS is driven and resilient
They are admired and inspire others
They defy the odds to win
They mind their business
They take care of their people

So, I conclude with the reasons I wrote this book. 2020 was a defining year that cast a light on inequities, lack of knowledge, and funding that continues to limit our growth. For more than 100 million small women and minority-owned businesses, job creation, economic impact in minority communities need to be more aggressive. A monumental need is to understand advanced business principles to step out of our small thinking and learn BIG, bold strategies for serious revenue growth.

Leading like a BOSS is the action behind the dream, the vision, and the compass that steers the course to reach our goals.

When we grow internally, we prosper and grow externally

A BOSS recognizes the ebbs and flows of leading, elevating, and celebrating wins and learning from the losses.

Here's my challenge to you: join me in building BOSS communities in our hometowns, cities, and around the world to inspire the growth of more millionaire and billionaire companies that offer high-paying jobs, impact economic development in underserved and rural communities, and change economic policies that limit wealth building and community stability.

A *BOSS* - We are **B**uilt **o**n **S**piritual **S**trength

www.ingramcontent.com/pod-product-compliance
Lightning Source LLC
LaVergne TN
LVHW041630060526
838200LV00040B/1520